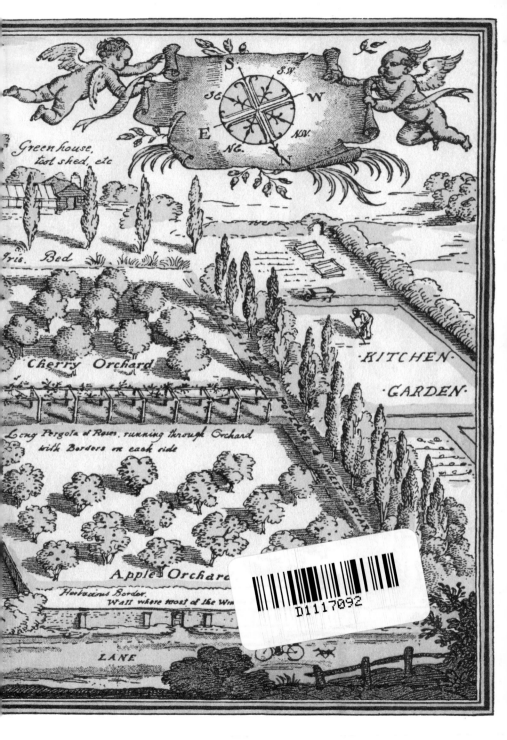

Greenhouse, tool shed, etc

Iris Bed

Cherry Orchard

Long Pergola of Roses, running through Orchard with Borders on each side

KITCHEN
GARDEN

Apple Orchard

Herbaceous Border.
Wall where most of the Wm

LANE

DOWN THE
GARDEN PATH

Beverley Nichols's Thatch Cottage at Glatton, photographed at the height of summer. Courtesy of the Bryan Connon Collection.

DOWN THE GARDEN PATH

by
BEVERLEY NICHOLS

With a Foreword by
BRYAN CONNON

TIMBER PRESS
Portland • London

Dust jacket photograph of Beverley Nichols
and frontispiece photograph of Thatch Cottage at Glatton
are the property of Bryan Connon, reproduced with permission.

Drawings by Rex Whistler

Copyright © 1932 by the Estate of Beverley Nichols.
All rights reserved.

First published in 1932 by Jonathan Cape
Foreword and Index copyright © 2005 by Timber Press, Inc.

Published in 2005 by

Timber Press, Inc.
The Haseltine Building
133 S.W. Second Avenue, Suite 450
Portland, Oregon 97204-3527
timberpress.com

2 The Quadrant
135 Salusbury Road
London NW6 6RJ
timberpress.co.uk.

Seventh printing 2013
ISBN-13: 978-0-88192-710-8
Printed in the United States of America

Catalog records for this book are available from the Library of
Congress and the British Library.

CONTENTS

Foreword by Bryan Connon   vii

Down the Garden Path
Facsimile of the original edition of 1932   4
Contents   7

Index by Roy C. Dicks   291

v

FOREWORD

To those of you who already know *Down the Garden Path*, rereading it will be like returning to an old and trusted friend. If it is new to you there are, I promise, unexpected pleasures to relish. As the Gardening Club of America declared in 1932, "it is one of the most delectable and diverting garden books ever published." It remains unique despite many attempts by optimistic authors to imitate it, but none has been able to capture the qualities that made it an international success.

In the 1920s Beverley Nichols appeared to be the epitome of the jazz-age playboy: handsome, elegant and witty, often posing languidly, a cigarette in one hand and a cocktail in the other. He knew everyone and everyone knew him. He counted among his male friends Cole Porter, Noel Coward, Somerset Maugham and among the ladies: Gloria Swanson, Anita Loos (who wrote *Gentlemen Prefer Blondes*) and the great opera soprano Dame Nellie Melba—whose autobiography he ghosted—as well as a host of others from every strata of society. To the general public he seemed dedicated to the endless pursuit of pleasure. As he put it, "It was the same old routine day after day, night after night—talking incessantly, laughing a lot, with the cocktail shaker keeping up a perpetual staccato accompaniment in the background." But he was unfair to himself, for by the time he was thirty his output was prodigious; the plays, music, essays, short stories and novels he wrote would have satisfied the ambitions of most individuals for a lifetime. However, he was highly self-critical and had begun to hate the superficiality of the playboy image he had created for the public. The turning point came almost by chance, but it was to change both his personal and professional lives.

The story began in Chicago in 1918, when he was a lowly army lieutenant seconded as secretary to an English goodwill mission to America. At the home of the millionaire Ryerson family he was befriended by Mrs. Emily Borie Ryerson and her brother John Borie. He subsequently stayed with Borie at his home in the village of Glatton, England, a picture-postcard Tudor cottage built in 1520 with a flower-packed garden. He never forgot it, and when Borie died Beverley bought the property from Mrs. Ryerson in 1928, intending to use it as an occasional weekend retreat. But he was unaware that it had been badly neglected, and it was nearly a year later when he returned from working in New York that he saw its shocking state. Fortunately Beverley's father was able to supervise clearing the garden and restoring the cottage. Beverley helped when he could escape his London home, where he was working on a new musical show for the impresario C. B. Cochran, a play called "The Stag," finishing a book, and writing regularly for the press! Despite this frenetic work schedule, his head was filled with ambitious plans for the garden, and to carry these out he doubled its size by acquiring more land. As Noel Coward once remarked, "amateurs have no fear," and Beverley proved him right by going ahead, often against expert advice and with disastrous results. For example, he planted a grove of twenty mimosas in the depth of winter in a cold, windswept field under a protective tent of muslin. A sudden snowstorm covered the tent and brought it crashing down, snapping the slender stems of the plants, and the bitter wind did the rest. He then had more problems with the grove he had planted, as the trees died for no apparent reason. It was his father who suggested a lack of drainage was causing the trees to become waterlogged. Investigation proved him right, and he organized a new system of field drains which prevented further losses. Beverley's enthusiasm was undimmed by these setbacks, and eventually his successes outweighed his failures. He was particularly proud of his triumph with winter aconites, which were virtually unknown to the average gardener at the time. He dubbed them "the buttercups of February," and this description was adopted by dealers when they began to include them in their catalogues.

Beverley was, of course, no stranger to gardens but never before acted as an active participant in the cultivation. Both sides of his family were well-to-do folk, and he and his brothers were used to large houses surrounded by spacious grounds kept in order by the outdoor staff. The style was heavily influenced by the splendid municipal gardens which were the pride of every local authority in Britain; hedges were neatly clipped, lawns rolled and cut into submission and flowers lined up like rows of military men on ceremonial parade. Beautiful as these formal Victorian gardens were, Beverley was also enchanted by the cottage gardens he glimpsed on walks with his governess. He was attracted to their happy chaos of rambling roses and honeysuckle and flowerbeds which were crammed with every sort of old-fashioned bloom. Consequently in his designs, he combined the virtues of cottage gardens with the formality of the gardens of his childhood.

He was never one to miss a writing opportunity, and it occurred to him that a book based on his experiences as playboy-turned-gardener might amuse his readers. It took him less than three weeks to finish it. As he said, "It was hardly like writing a book at all; it was more like arranging a bunch of mixed flowers." The result was a cunning blend of fact and fiction combined with pathos, humour and charm. He called it *Down the Garden Path*, and he anticipated modest sales when it came out in 1932; contrary to expectations it was an astonishing success and made publishing history.

The finishing touch to it was the contribution by Rex Whistler, a brilliant young artist whom Beverley insisted should be employed to illustrate the book. The results speak for themselves. The happy collaboration was to continue with the successors to *Down the Garden Path*, *A Thatched Roof* (1933) and *A Village in a Valley* (1934), which allowed Beverley to expand his cast of notable characters and gave scope to Whistler's imagination. (Whistler was tragically killed leading a counterattack near Caen only weeks before the World War II ended in 1945.)

Beverley was frequently asked whether the characters he introduced in *Down the Garden Path* were "real." Some, like his father, were real enough, but others were fictionalised versions of people he knew. Miss Hazlitt, for example, was based on his governess Meig Herridge, who played an important part in his childhood development. It was she who taught him, in addition to "reading, writing and arithmetic," the Latin names of flowers which, once learned, he never forgot. The model for the Professor was his old friend A. M. Low, a distinguished scientist. "Mrs. M." made such an impact that Beverley's publishers used to receive letters addressed to her asking for advice! Arthur, who makes a brief appearance at the beginning of the book, was based on an unsatisfactory servant Beverley once employed. Students of the English social scene in the 1930s will note that Beverley did not sack him personally, but sent his "man" to get rid of him. This was Gaskin, who was the factotum in charge of Beverley's London house in Westminster and who later featured in several books. There is also a mysterious mention of an unnamed American. It puzzled many readers because he appears only once and then vanishes from the story. This was Warren, whom Beverley hoped would become a lifelong companion but who returned to New York when he could not adjust to life in England, away from the glitter of Manhattan.

Readers were also curious about Beverley's choice of "Allways" as a substitute name for Glatton, where Thatch Cottage is situated. He was inspired by Irving Berlin's hit song of 1925, "Always." It was an apt choice, for the song celebrated love, and Beverley's love for Glatton and all it represented lasted all his life. When he died in 1983 his ashes were scattered on the grounds of the old village church as he had requested. It would have pleased him if this informal ceremony could have taken place in the garden he had designed, but, as he had discovered years before, its characters had been completely altered after he left the village.

Shortly before his death I called on him one afternoon at his final home, Sudbrook Cottage. After tea he asked me to help him to his favourite garden seat where he could enjoy the vista. There had been no garden worthy of the term when he first bought the cottage; most of it was a rough grass field, which had once been a paddock for working horses. Out of this bare stretch of ground he had created a garden of which he was justifiably proud and which now looked splendid in the August sunshine. Although illness had made him very frail, there was no sign of age in his voice as we chatted about incidents in his life for inclusion in the biography which he had asked me to write. On previous occasions we had discussed *Down the Garden Path,* due to be republished to celebrate its 50th anniversary. "Back in 1932 I was mocked by a few who dismissed my interest in gardening as the passing fancy of a flibbertigibbet and the book as worthless nonsense doomed to failure." He paused and then smiled, "How wrong they proved to be!"

Happy reading!

BRYAN CONNON
Eastbourne, Sussex

DOWN THE GARDEN PATH

by
BEVERLEY NICHOLS

with Decorations by
REX WHISTLER

Facsimile of the original edition of 1932

DOWN THE GARDEN PATH

By Beverley Nichols

· LONDON ·

Jonathan Cape

CONTENTS

	FOREWORD	9
I	THE GARDEN GATE	15
II	ARTHUR	21
III	SALVAGE	35
IV	MID-WINTER MADNESS	51
V	MORE WINTER FLOWERS	68
VI	GARDEN FRIENDS	80
VII	GARDEN ENEMIES	94
VIII	HOW NOT TO MAKE A ROCK GARDEN	104
IX	THE OTHER SIDE OF THE PICTURE	113
X	MIRACLES	132
XI	THE EDGE OF THE WOOD	151
XII	IN THE WOOD	174
XIII	THE PROFESSOR	188
XIV	THE GREENHOUSE	209
XV	WOMEN GARDENERS	227
XVI	AND YET	243
XVII	BOUQUET	258
XVIII	A NOTE ON LONDON GARDENS	269
	EPILOGUE	287

FOREWORD

I believe in doing things too soon. In striking before the iron is hot, in leaping before one has looked, in loving before one has been introduced. Nearly all the great and exciting things in life have been done by men who did them too soon. It was far, far too soon for Columbus to set out on his crazy trip to the New World. The ether was not ready for Beethoven when he began a symphony on a dominant seventh. Shelley, long before the appointed time, unloosed, with trembling fingers, the starched ribbons which bound the dress of Poetry. 'Too soon . . . too soon . . .' it is the snarling sleepy cry which greets all new-born beauty, all flights of the spirit.

I know that unless I write a gardening book now . . . swiftly, and finish it before the last bud outside my window has spread its tiny fan . . . it will be too late to write it at all. For shortly I shall know too much . . . shall dilate, with tedious prolixity, on the root formation of the winter aconite, instead of trying to catch on paper the glint of its gold through the snow, as I remember it last winter, like a fistful of largesse thrown over a satin quilt. Just as the best school stories are written by boys who have only just left school, so, I feel, the best gardening books should be written by those who still have to search their brains for the honeysuckle's languid Latin name, who still feel awe at the miracle which follows the setting of a geranium cutting in its appointed loam.

That is why I have written this book. You must not look to it for guidance. It will not tell you how to prune a rose-bush, nor will it suddenly explode with terrifying remarks like 'Now is the time to thin out the carrots . . .' . . . an observation which always makes me come out in a cold sweat, when I read it in a London paper. As though the earth were hardening, minute by minute, so that one must rush up to the country and do things before it is too late.

No . . . I fear that this book holds little practical wisdom. But if any gardeners should honour me by turning its pages, idly, after their day's work is done, I hope that from time to time they may be tempted to smile, not unkindly, at the recollection of their own early follies. And I hope that there may come to them, once more, a faint tremor of that first ecstasy which shook them when they learnt that a garden is the only mistress who never fails, who never fades. . .

To Marie Rose Antoinette Catherine de Robert
d'Aqueria de Rochegude d'Erlanger
whose charms are as gay
and numerous as
her names

¶ A few extracts from this book have appeared in *Country Life* to whose editor I am happy to make the customary acknowledgements

DOWN THE
GARDEN PATH

CHAPTER I

THE GARDEN GATE

§ 1

I BOUGHT my cottage by sending a wireless to Timbuctoo from the *Mauretania*, at midnight, with a fierce storm lashing the decks.

It sounds rather vulgar, but it is true. The cottage used to belong to a charming American, whom I knew very slightly. I read of his death in a paper which I picked up in the stuffy, pitching library of the aforesaid vessel. It told me that Mr. So-and-So had died, and that he had left all his property to his sister . . . who was one of my best friends.

The liner dipped and tossed. I studied the paper. I saw that Wall Street, the night before, had been giving one of its celebrated impersonations of the fall of Jericho. People had been leaping from the tops of skyscrapers with monotonous regularity. Nothing seemed stable in this world. And then, looking again at the little obituary notice of this man whom I had scarcely known, I remembered that among his possessions had been an exquisite thatched cottage, where I had once spent a week-end. The garden had been a blaze of roses, and there was a row of madonna lilies on either side of the porch. The scent of those lilies assailed me. I reached for a piece of paper, scribbled the name of the American's sister, and the word Timbuctoo, whither she had ventured on a wild excursion. I rang the bell and wrote an offer. As the page boy took my cablegram, I scratched two hundred pounds from the sum I had proposed. He had hardly left the lounge before I tried to call him back, for I regretted the whole idea. But he was gone, and the night was very stormy indeed, and the decks were dark and slippery. Before I could reach the wireless operator's headquarters, the message was sent.

Thank God for that storm at sea. My offer was accepted. Within a week I was driving through the quiet lanes, towards my inheritance.

§ 11

I usually skip topographical details in novels. The more elaborate the description of the locality, the more confused does my mental impression become. You know the sort of thing: —

'Jill stood looking out of the door of her cottage. To the North rose the vast peak of Snowdon. To the South swept the valley, dotted with fir trees. Beyond the main ridge of mountains a pleasant wooded country extended itself, but the

nearer slopes were scarred and desolate. Miles below a thin ribbon of river wound towards the sea, which shone, like a distant shield, beyond the etc. etc.'

By the time I have read a little of this sort of thing I feel dizzy. Is Snowdon in front or behind? Are the woods to the right or to the left. The mind makes frenzied efforts to carry it all, without success. It would be very much better if the novelist said 'Jill stood on the top of a hill, and looked down into the valley below.' And left it at that.

But in a book of this class — you really must get topographical details in your head. You will be walking through my garden, from the first pale mists of spring to the urgent, stormy nights of November. You will be shading your eyes from the sun under arches that reel with the intoxicating scent of syringa, and hurrying through the little French windows to escape the menace of the blue-black clouds of April. It is vital, therefore, that you know where you are going, or you will trip up. You will forget the step that comes before the lupin bed, and crack your head on a branch of the damson tree.

Therefore, soon we will draw a plan. But first of all, we must take a wider view.

If you look at the map you will find, somewhere towards the centre of England, a county called Huntingdonshire. There is no smaller county in the land, except Rutlandshire, which is really so small that it is no longer funny. There is no county more essentially English than Huntingdonshire. If you go

into its sleepy little capital and drink a bitter at one of
the little inns, you will find farmers who speak with a
dialect which would have sounded familiar to Pepys,
who had a cottage in the neighbourhood. The poor
devils are mostly bankrupt now. They stand at the
doors of their inns, looking out with puzzled eyes at
the great charabancs that sweep by from Newcastle
. . . down the same Great North Road which once
echoed to the hoofs of Dick Turpin's horse, on clear
frosty nights.

The village in which my cottage is situated is called
. . . well, Allways is as good a name as any other.
It is not unlike its real name. And it is not inap-
propriate. . . . All Ways. For though it lies a mile
from the Great North Road, there is a tangle of white,
winding country roads that meet and lace and part
again, at its village green, running from haven to
haven, over hills and valleys that seem to have been
forsaken by the rest of the world.

On the wall over one of my staircases . . . (I have
three staircases, and no man can decide which is the
smallest) . . . there is a map, dated A.D. 1576. It is a
very beautiful map. Two cherubs, in the last stages
of elephantiasis, spread gilt and bloated limbs over its
pale parchment. A crown, a turtle, a stork, a dragon,
a bunch of pears . . . and many delicious scrolls and
devices, touched with blue and scarlet, are scattered
over the widely painted acres. In the right hand
bottom corner there is a lion, rampant . . . oh, most
exceedingly rampant, with a scroll that comes from
his mouth, on which are written the words *Pestis*

Patria Pigricies. If you have the faintest idea what that means, you are to be congratulated. There is a sound of the plague about it, and for all I know, the sound may have an echo of sense, for the land round the cottage is low lying . . . and the fields, in November, are the scene of many strange sarabandes, as the mists drift over the willows, pause, curve, drift nearer . . . But I would not have it changed.

Often, as I have carried my lonely candle to bed, I have paused and studied this enchanting document. The candlelight gleams and flickers on the dragon and the tortoise and the stork . . . many pale points of gilt glitter through the glass . . . as perhaps they glittered, three hundred and fifty years ago, for other natives of this dear stretch of earth. I explore, in a fine sweep, the flat lands from Cambridge to Stamford . . . which in those days was spelt with an N . . . I see the grey marshes which have long been filled in . . . the faded, formal bunches of trees which have long been cut down . . . I see the proud flourishes over Huntingdon, whose head, then, was so highly lifted. And finally, with a catch of the breath, I put the candle closer, and read, with a quite unjustified sense of proprietorship . . . the word Allways. There is a little green mill-sign above it, and a cross for a church. There is also a tiny speck which I try to persuade myself is my cottage. But it is to be feared that it is only the mark of a very old-fashioned beetle.

We are hurrying towards the garden gate, and in a moment we shall be able to lift the latch. But there is one final introduction to be made . . . the cottage itself.

It stands on the road . . . a very quiet road. It is thatched with reed, and heavily timbered, with beams that have been twisted, by Time, into lovely shapes. It is really three cottages, knocked into one, which explains the phenomenon of the three staircases. There is a little patch of grass outside which is filled to the brim with crocuses, white and yellow for spring, and mauve for autumn. People say the sight of the crocuses, blazing away in March and September, is one of the prettiest things a man could see. They are right.

My cottage is much bigger than you would think, from the outside. This is as it should be. For you alight at the tiny front door, and look up at this charming old box of a place, and then, on entering, you find an unsuspected wing, hidden from the road by a thick bank of may and lilac, and when you get into this wing you step out into a secret garden, and behind the secret garden . . . But here we are, with the latch not only lifted but the garden gate swinging wide, and the whole thread of the narrative lost. I must get back quickly, to the beginning, to that evening in early April when I jostled along the country road in the village Ford, prepared for Paradise.

CHAPTER II

ARTHUR

§ 1

BEFORE leaving London, on this day of days, I had been to the solicitors, to make sure that everything was in order, and that the cottage was really mine. A few last-minute documents had been signed, a few more pounds paid. And then, as I was about to take my leave, the solicitor said:

'I hope you'll like Arthur.'

'Arthur?'

'Yes . . . the man we put in as gardener-caretaker, on the decease of the former owner.'

'I'm sure he's charming,' I said. 'Is he very large?'

'How do you mean?'

'I should prefer him to be large. In the country, you know.'

'I don't know if he's large. But he's local.'

'Then he's probably enormous. Huntingdon is famous for giants.'

'Really? I didn't know that.'

Neither did I. But I was already swelling with the pride of the landed proprietor.

The solicitor told me that Arthur was a good plain cook and an excellent gardener, and that he would certainly be able to 'do' for me until I got a 'man and his wife.'

'He's been there for six months, so he ought to have got the place pretty ship-shape.'

I assented quickly, and hurried off to catch my train. As the train hurried through the fields, I remembered the charming old couple who had been keeping house on my previous visit. If Arthur was half as good as they had been all should be well.

§ 11

A narrow lane, that twists and turns, directs you from the Great North Road to the village of Allways. It is seldom that one meets any traffic on it. A startled child, pressing back into the hedge with exaggerated caution as you pass . . . a woman on a bicycle with a floppy, old-fashioned hat and a curved back . . . an occasional farm cart, which can only be passed with great ingenuity and many amiable sallies. For the rest, the only other occupants of the road are the rabbits, which are legion. In the spring there are many young ones, so pathetically innocent and silly that sometimes it is necessary to stop the car, dismount, and speak quite rudely to them before they are so obliging as to run away. At night their eyes glow with phosphorescent fire and sometimes they are hypnotized by the lights of the car, so that one must pull up, and turn out the lights, in order that they may recover their self-possession. Very pleasant are those little halts, in the dark, with the wind playing in the high trees above, and the rain dripping monotonously on the wind-screen.

ARTHUR

There were rabbits in plenty on the day that the car rattled down the lanes towards my inheritance, but I was too excited to be over-anxious about their welfare. Though I had only spent a single week-end in this place that was now my own I remembered the country-side as clearly as if I had lived in it for many seasons. The flat, quiet fields with their ancient willows that would so soon be feathered with green . . . the wide, meandering stream by the side of the road . . . the coppice of beech and chestnut with catkins swinging in the breeze . . . .

And now, the familiar bend in the road, the glimpse of a thatched roof, the sudden view of the white walls sturdily timbered. And it was mine . . . mine!

I jumped out of the Ford. My hand trembled violently as I paid the driver. The car turned, shunted and drove away. For a minute I stayed there in the road, staring at this beloved thing. It was difficult to realize that it was mine, from the top brick on the chimney to the grass at the foot of the walls. No . . . right down to the centre of the earth, and up to the heavens above, it was mine. But one cannot grasp these things as quickly as all that.

Then, as I stood there, I again remembered the existence of Arthur. Surely it was a little odd that nobody had come to greet me? I stepped across to the house and tried the door. It was bolted. I knocked, and waited. Who *was* Arthur? What was he like? Somehow I had assumed, as a matter of course, that he must be perfect.

My meditations were interrupted by the sight of a curious figure in the hall. It was a man in black, with a pale suspicious face. He was peering at me. Then he came to the door and opened it.

'Arthur?'

'I was expecting you.' His voice seemed to come from a very long way off. He spoke with a slight Irish accent.

It was on the tip of my tongue to say that if he was expecting me it was rather strange that he should not do something about it. However, I said nothing, partly because he had already glided away, leaving me with a suitcase in my hand, and partly because nothing could destroy the elation of these first few moments in my own home.

I shut the door, kicked the suitcase against the wall, and went through to the front room. One had to stoop to avoid the low beams. My heart was beating very quickly, because now, at last, I was to see again the garden of which I had so often dreamed.

§ III

I stepped through the window. Stopped dead. Blinked . . . Looked again . . . and the spirit seemed to die within me.

It was a scene of utter desolation. True, it was a cold evening in late March, and the shadows were falling. No garden can be expected to look its best in such circumstances. But this garden did not look like a garden at all. There was not even a sense of

24

order about it. All design was lacking. Even in the grimmest winter days a garden can give an appearance of discipline, and a certain amount of life and colour, no matter how wild the winds nor dark the skies. But this garden was like a rubbish heap.

In my mind's eye there had glowed a brilliant bouquet of flowers. I cherished the memory of beds that had glowed like the drunken canvas of an impressionist painter. I recalled arches weighed down with their weight of burning blossom. Through my mind there still drifted the languid essences of July, a summer halo encircled me and. . .

And now? Nothing. Earth. Sodden grass. Rank bushes. A wind that cut one to the marrow. I shivered.

Then I pulled myself together. It was unreasonable, surely, to be shocked by this prospect. One could not expect summer glory in the middle of winter.

But this mood did not last for long. For it was *not* the middle of winter. It was the beginning of spring. One knew enough poetical tags to be aware that daffodils took the winds of March, that snowdrops had been nicknamed the 'fair maids of February,' that more than one poet had chronicled the advent of the primrose. But here was no daffodil, no snowdrop, no primrose.

I pulled the collar of my coat up and strode into the garden. Everywhere, there was the evidence of appalling neglect. Ignorant as I was of all the technicalities, I knew, at least, that good gardeners did not leave the old shoots of pruned roses lying on the ground. The roses seemed to have been pruned in the autumn, and the cuttings left on the beds through the winter. Nor did good gardeners allow hedges to grow apace, nor let ivy trail up the stems of young trees, nor permit the paths and borders to be swallowed up by ugly weeds. Why — there were even old newspapers lying sodden in the orchard!

I was just turning over one of these newspapers with a stick when there was the sound of a footstep behind me. I turned and saw Arthur only a few paces away. How he had come so near without making any sound, I cannot imagine. Still, there he was. He had pale watery eyes, and drooping shoulders. He smelt strongly of gin. His hands hung straight down by his side.

'Oh . . . Arthur . . .'

'Yes sir?' He spoke as though he were drugged.

'The garden seems a little . . .' I paused. I am terribly bad at 'telling people off' — especially if they are in a subservient position. So I concluded weakly . . . 'there seems a good deal to be done here.'

'There is, sir. Far more than one man could do by 'imself.'

'I wouldn't say that.'

'No sir, but then . . . you 'aven't 'ad much to do with gardens before, 'ave you?'

The sly insolence of the remark cut me. I looked him straight in his horrible watery eyes. I said:

'As far as I can see you haven't had much to do with gardens, either. At any rate you haven't had much to do with this one. . . .'

I will not humiliate either myself or the reader with a further recital of this discussion. There is always something a little degrading in the disagreements of master and man, or of mistress and maid. The dice are always loaded so heavily in favour of the employer.

I returned to the cottage, and drew the blinds. I wanted to shut it all out. I sat down and lit a cigarette. It was evident that a great deal of work lay before me.

Such was the garden, when I entered into my inheritance.

§ IV

I finished my cigarette, lit another, and another. Gradually I worked myself up into a fury against Arthur. For six months he had been here, with nothing to do . . . no tenants . . . no extra work of any kind, and all the assistance that he chose to command. This was the result! I would sack him in the morning. This was my virtuous resolve.

I have not properly described Arthur. He was very heavy-lidded and pasty faced. He had no chin. He crept about the house in the oddest way, touching ornaments with his hands and breathing heavily. He smiled, slyly, in corners.

Yet, here was I, at his mercy. For the first time in my life I understood the reality of 'the servant problem.' I had always thought that women had invented this problem. But no woman on earth could have coped with the inefficiency, the laziness and the malice of Arthur.

I sat down in the lonely little dining-room. The lamp flickered and cast strange shadows on the ceiling. The wind howled and the rain lashed the windows. Arthur crept into the room with two plates, which he deposited on the table in front of me. Then he crept out again, hissing slightly.

To this day I do not know what it was that he had concocted. It looked like some form of meat, and it had about it the horrible smell of poverty . . . the smell of the slums. There were some potatoes in the other dish . . . 'mashed'. They were bright yellow, and he had decorated them with an awful design by digging them with a fork. I gulped with disgust, and swallowed a whisky and soda. Then I took the plates and tiptoed to the window. I opened it. A bitter wind blew in, almost extinguishing the lamps. I threw the whole hideous business into the bushes. I could have sworn that there was a shower of acid-green sparks as the meat hit the earth. . . .

§ v

The next morning I woke at about half-past nine. The sun was streaming into the room, and I felt at peace with the world. The supernatural tendencies of Arthur seemed less threatening. I thought I would give him another trial.

I rang the bell. It echoed away into the distance. I lay and waited. There was no reply. I rang again. Still no reply. This was very odd. I clambered out of bed, and put on a dressing-gown. Before going downstairs I looked out of the window. In the hard yellow sunlight it seemed more desolate than ever. Even the earth appeared stony and sterile as though it would never again bear fruit.

I shivered, and clambered down the little uneven staircase. The hall was bitterly cold. As I looked into the sitting room I saw that no fire had been lit.

Here I must pause, for a moment, to record the fact that I am, as a rule, an even-tempered person. But there is a period when I cannot easily be trifled with. And that period is before breakfast.

Picture me, therefore, standing in a draughty passage leading to the kitchen. At the end of the passage there is a sink, into which a tap drips monotonously. This is the only sound, save the rumbling of my own stomach. And the echo of my voice as I cry, for the tenth time:

'Arthur!'

At last there is a sign of life. A creaking door. A streak of light. Arthur appears in a dressing-gown. A dressing-gown which looked as though it should have been worn by an emaciated gigolo on one of his least successful week-ends. A dressing-gown that could not possibly be associated with Allways.

'You called?'

I am struck all of a heap, as they say. Of course I called. Is it not half-past nine? And are not servants, by the laws of Nature, up and about long before half-past nine?

'Certainly I called. It is half-past nine.'

'As late as that?' He blinked owlishly. I felt
if I studied him in detail I should see a lot of unpleasant things that I preferred not to see. So I
merely regarded him through half-closed lids and
said, in stilted, artificial tones:

'I would like breakfast at once, please. And I would
be glad if you would go over the garden with me
at ten o'clock.'

§ VI

I did not get breakfast for an hour. Incredible as it
sounds, it is true. And I did not go over the garden
with him at all.

When, at last, Arthur condescended to bring me
something to eat — (in normal circumstances it
would have been uneatable) — he casually informed
me that he 'was not feeling very well and he had
decided to go back to bed.'

I should have hit him, of course. I should have
taken huge rocks, and crushed them on to his stomach.
But I was feeling faint with hunger and too hysterical
to formulate an adequate protest. So I merely nodded,
registered loathing, and swallowed my tea, and went
out for a walk.

In the lane I met Mrs. M., a middle-aged woman
with a hard jaw. I had been introduced to her on my
previous visit. She lives in a very perfect cottage not
many miles away. She will recur through these
pages, with irritating frequency. She is never ill,
never fooled, never at a loss. She makes a pound do

the work of a fiver, and her garden is maddeningly efficient. She despises me, in her heart of hearts, but puts up with me because I subscribe to things.

She was striding down the lane with a horribly well-bred terrier, which had legs as straight as corn stalks, and a predatory look in its eyes. As soon as she saw me she halted, dug her stick in the ground, sat on it, and greeted me as follows:

'Ha! So the Lord of the Manor's arrived.'

I muttered something inaudible.

'And how many chapters have you written this morning?'

'None,' I snapped. 'I've only just had breakfast.'

'*What?* But it's nearly twelve o'clock.'

'I know. But my man seems to dislike getting up before ten.'

Mrs. M's eyes gleamed with delight. '*No!* You don't mean to tell me . . . ten? Impossible!'

I disliked the evident relish with which she received this titbit of news, but I had to unburden my grievances to somebody.

'It *is* impossible, isn't it? I mean, I'm not being unreasonable, or anything like that? I mean . . . really, he only has to look after the house, because he gets heaps of help in the garden.'

'Unreasonable!' She said it with such vehemence that she slightly but unmistakably spat over my left shoulder. She knew that she had spat, and she knew that *I* knew that she had spat, but she was not in the least abashed. She merely made a genteel scraping noise in her throat, and repeated the word 'unreasonable!' Though this time, for safety's sake, she said it through half closed lips, and added:

'*Why* doesn't he get up?'

'I really don't know.'

'But what excuse did he give?'

'He said he didn't realize the time.' Then I added my crowning tit-bit. 'He's gone back to bed at this moment.'

'Gone back — to — bed?' she gasped. 'But . . . but.'

'He said he didn't feel very well.'

'I have never — no never — heard of such a thing. Not feel very well! Why my Hawkins. . . .'

'Your what?'

'My maid Hawkins . . . been with me twenty-seven years . . . she would rise from her death-bed rather than that I should miss my morning cup of tea.' (Even in the heat of the moment, this struck me as a little unreasonable.) 'From her death-bed,' repeated Mrs. M. 'She has *never* failed to get up at a quarter to six. By a quarter to seven all the fires are made and lit, and the two sitting rooms thoroughly dusted. By half-past seven her own room is done, and everything prepared for breakfast, and she brings me my morning tea. By eight. . . .'

'Yes, yes. . .' I interrupted. 'But what am I to do about Arthur?'

'You must give him notice at once.'

'But suppose he stays in bed and refuses to get up at all?'

'How could he?'

32

'He could with the very greatest ease', I replied warmly.

'But what does he *do* in bed?' asked Mrs. M.

And then she suddenly realized that her question was 'one of those things which might have been phrased differently.'

§ VII

I departed that afternoon without saying good-bye to Arthur. I felt sick and disheartened, as though I never wanted to see the place again. When I got home I explained the situation to my servant, and told him that he must go up on the following morning and give him notice, and that he must not return until he was out of the house. I gave him a month's wages in cash, with which to pacify the brute.

He left at ten in the morning. To my astonishment, he returned the same night.

'Well . . .' I demanded, 'what happened? Why have you come back?'

'He's gone, sir.'

'Gone? Already? Wasn't he in bed?'

'He was in bed, sir.'

'Well. . .?'

And then I desisted. I realized that a miracle had been accomplished, and that it was not for me to enquire how it had been accomplished. But I still allow myself to dream about it, now and then, to visualize the slim disdainful figure of my servant picking his way delicately through the country lanes

C

33

. . . to imagine him entering the kitchen, sniffing at the dirt and confusion of it all, knocking peremptorily at the bedroom door, entering, and haughtily ejecting the loathsome occupant of the bed. . . .

Well, that is all a thing of the past. A few weeks after the departure of Arthur the S's arrived. They are with me still, and I sincerely hope that they will be with me always.

CHAPTER III

SALVAGE

§ 1

AND now the work of salvage began. There were tools to be ordered, a wheelbarrow to be bought, beds to be filled with roses, hedges to be clipped, bushes to be uprooted. The greenhouse had to be patched up, the tool-shed wanted a new roof. We had to decide on a place for a rubbish heap, to fix the limits of the kitchen garden. We had to rush about with quantities of manure, pushing it into the ground with a feeling of supreme benefaction. We had to get weed-killer (the non-poisonous sort), and sprinkle it on the overgrown paths. We had to leap with heavy hatred upon ants' nests and squash the brutes, which were over-running the whole garden. We had to burn, and destroy and ravage before we could really create. And the extraordinary thing about it was that gradually my impatient desire for immediate results, which is the besetting sin of all beginners, died down. I began to take a joy in the work for its own sake.

Until you actually *own* a garden, you cannot know this joy. You may say 'oh yes, I love a garden.' But what do you really mean by that? You mean that you like to wander through rows of hollyhocks, swathed in tulle . . . (you, not the hollyhocks), and that you like to drink lemonade under a tree with a

35

nice young man who will shortly pick you a large bunch of roses. You hope he will take the thorns off, and that there will not be any earwigs in them, because if you found an earwig on the rug in the car you would die with horror. (So should I.)

You like walking out on to a terrace and looking up at a wall that is covered with the pale, tipsy plumes of wistaria . . . to walk under arches of orange blossom, thinking the prettiest thoughts . . . and you may even stoop down to pick a bunch of pansies, if they match your frock. You like these things, yes.

But you do not like grovelling on the earth in search of a peculiarly nauseating slug that has been eating those pansies. You do not like putting a trowel under the slug, hoping that it will not suddenly burst or produce fearful slime, and tipping the slug with gratified horror into a basket. You do not like bending down for hours to pull up hateful little weeds that break off above the root . . . (not groundsel, because groundsel is a lovely weed to pull up) . . . but small docks and wretched things like that. You do not like these things, for one reason and only one reason . . . because you do not *own* the garden.

All gardeners will know what I mean. Ownership makes all the difference in the world. I suppose it is like the difference between one's own baby and somebody else's. If it is your own baby you probably quite enjoy wiping its nose. If it is somebody else's you would have to use a long pole with a handkerchief on the end . . . at least I should.

That was why I loved all this early work, because

36

the garden was the first thing I had ever really owned. It took ages to realize it . . . to this day the realization is not complete. I still stand before a hedge with a pair of shears in my hand, saying 'I can clip this hedge exactly as I please. I can make it round or square or like a castle. If I choose, I can clip it away altogether, and nobody can arrest me.'

To dig one's own spade into one's own earth! Has life anything better to offer than this?

§11

Very soon, we shall be able to be far more definite, to deal with actual facts, to scatter hints, to tell stories with a certain amount of plot in them. But at the moment, I find, in writing this book, that I am up against the same difficulty which confronted me when I wrote my first book. That was a school story called *Prelude*. It still brings me a large weekly correspondence from wistful boys in Colonial swamps.

The difficulty one has in writing a school story is that nothing ever happens at school. (Nothing, I mean, that one could possibly print in anything but a German Nature magazine.) Of course, there *are* school stories in which things happen with almost breathless speed . . . prefects forge cheques, large boys rescue small boys from burning buildings, and housemasters' wives are seduced by members of the lower school before they have had time to say 'Jack' . . . which is the word they usually do say, in ever tenderer accents, as the story proceeds. However, nothing like that ever happened in *my* school, so that

I had to content myself by drawing a pretty picture of the gradual burgeoning of my young soul. Perhaps that is why the masters at Marlborough still refer to *Prelude* as 'scurrilous literature.'

A garden is like a school . . . it is a place of youth perpetually renewed . . . it arouses the same loyalties . . . it teaches the same lessons. Yet nothing really happens in it. Nothing 'novelistic'. A delphinium does not suddenly leap out of the herbaceous border and explode. A lilac bush does not, without warning, make rude noises behind one's back. What I am trying to express is that I cannot begin it all with a flourish . . . I cannot tell you that I went out one night, wide-eyed, with my hands full of seed, and sowed it, and lo! in the morning there was a field of blood-red poppies. Nothing like that happened at all, and lo! it would be a blood-red lie if I ever suggested that it did.

Yet just as a school is a place of slowly-expanding minds, of quiet adolescent dreams, of the play and inter-play of sweet friendship, so is a garden, whose story must be told with the delicacy of a leaf unfolding, in a soft, sighing prose that has the rise and fall of blowing branches. A pretty task to set oneself! Especially since my very first job must be the inevitably dreary one of describing the topography of my garden.

§ I I I

Topography in a garden book corresponds to genealogy in a novel. The best genealogist in fiction was Anthony Trollope. He had a gift for making his readers take a deep breath, swallow, and then glue themselves to his early pages until they knew everybody's aunts, uncles and cousins much better than they knew their own.

Would that I had this gift in such a book as I am writing! For I want you, so much, to know the way the paths run, to be aware that you must bend your head under this bough to avoid the sparkling raindrops, and step high, on a dark evening, as you enter the little box garden, so that you may not trip up. I fear that the gift is not mine, so that in a moment we shall have to show you a plan of it all . . . and I think that a plan is as tiresome as a family tree. Yet, it is necessary. How, otherwise, can we make The Tour?

Let me explain. Whenever I arrive in my garden, I Make The Tour. Is this a personal idiosyncracy, or do all good gardeners do it? It would be interesting to know. By Making The Tour, I mean only that I step from the front window, turn to the right, and make an infinitely detailed examination of every foot of ground, every shrub and tree, walking always over an appointed course.

There are certain very definite rules to be observed when you are Making The Tour. The chief rule is that you must never take anything out of its order. You may be longing to see if a crocus has come out in the orchard, but it is strictly forbidden to look before you have inspected all the various beds, bushes and trees that lead up to the orchard.

39

You must not look at the bed ahead before you have finished with the bed immediately in front of you. You may see, out of the corner of your eye, a gleam of strange and unsuspected scarlet in the next bed but one, but you must steel yourself against rushing to this exciting blaze, and you must stare with cool eyes at the earth in front, which is apparently blank, until you have made certain that it is not hiding anything. Otherwise you will find that you rush wildly round the garden, discover one or two sensational events, and then decide that nothing else has happened. Which means that you miss all the thrill of tiny shoots, the first lifting of the lids of the wallflowers, the first precious gold of the witch-hazel, the early spear of the snowdrop. Which recalls one of the loveliest conceits in English poetry, Coventry Patmore's line about the snowdrop. . . .

'And hails far summer with a lifted spear!'

It would require at least sixteen thick volumes bound in half calf, with bevelled edges, to contain a full account of a typical Tour round any garden. There is so much history in every foot of soil. So one can only hurry through it very briefly, to get the main outlines, and then draw a plan.

You step through some French windows into a small square garden, bordered with hedges of clipped blackthorn. Through the arch at the end is another garden, consisting of two big herbaceous borders, and a little circular lawn beyond. This gives straight on to some quiet fields, dotted with elms and oaks.

To the right, through another arch is an orchard, across which I have cut a path, edged with deep herbaceous borders. Beyond the orchard there is a coppice of poplars and sweet briar which hides the kitchen garden.

That is really all, except that there is a little Secret Garden on the other side of the house. It is only the size of a large room, and it is cut up into six box-edged beds filled with roses, and one large flower border, against a white wooden wall.

All of which leaves you, no doubt, in the same state of confusion as you were before. However, it had to be done. And at least, after this excursion, we shall have some justification for christening the various portions of the garden.

First comes the FRONT GARDEN. This is a very obvious title. In fact, its obviousness is its only claim to respect. It sounds prim and solid, like the front parlour. Which is what I try to make it. I like the flowers in it to be very well behaved, very formal, like glistening china ornaments on the mantelpiece of a house-proud woman.

The part beyond the Front Garden, through the aforesaid arch, we will call ANTINOUS' GARDEN. For I forgot to mention that there stands, in the centre of the little circular lawn, a statue of Antinous. I don't like garden ornaments, as a rule, especially in a humble garden like mine. I have a horror of those leaden cupids who illustrate, so gruesomely, the ultimate horrors of Bright's disease in many suburban pleasaunces. I cannot bear those grim terra cotta pelicans that peer sharply from thickets of bamboos in the grounds of tasteless Midland persons. I am depressed unutterably by those horrible little German manikins which some people scatter over their properties . . . grouping them oh! so archly . . . popping out of the rhododendrons, or lifting their horrid heads from a lavender hedge.

My Antinous, I feel, is of a different class. He is very beautiful, in himself. He once stood in the garden of an old house in Bedford Square. He was covered with grime and his limbs seemed stained eternally. I saw him first after lunch on a grey day of February. After shameless hinting and ogling I persuaded my host that he was unhappy in London, that it was not rain trickling from his pale eyes, but tears, that his feet were weary for the green grass. My host agreed. He really could do nothing else. It was ordained.

Antinous arrived in a crate, and was set in the centre of the little lawn. And gradually the sweet country rain washed his limbs, and the wind played about him. From his tired, worn fingers the grime departed, and his perfect, lyrical shoulders began to glisten in the sunlight. Now he shines and sparkles. He is spotless. To see him when the snow is on the ground, when the snowdrops are pushing humbly at his feet, when the winter sky is silver, white and blue . . . ah! that is to see man as a flower, yes, as a strange white flower.

There remains only the ORCHARD and the SECRET GARDEN which need no christening.

Here, therefore, we can draw the plan.

§ IV

At this point, the book begins. And it begins with mushrooms.

It is the very last thing that it should begin with, but we cannot help that. For I could not really tackle the flower garden till April, and then it was too late to do much more than get the soil in order, trim the hedges and discourage the more loathsome weeds. All these things took time. For the summer display I had to content myself with seedling stocks and antirrhinums, bought in boxes and pushed straight into the ground. (A degrading practice, this.) The first real experiment was with mushrooms, and like all first experiments in gardening, it was a failure.

One day I was walking in my large field looking for things. I was not looking for any particular thing — just things in the grass to pick or eat or play with. Then, over the fence, in a field that was not mine, I saw a mushroom. And I remembered glorious mushroom mornings in my boyhood, mornings when the long fingers of the sunlight were stretched flat on the fields. One had picked mushrooms then and had eaten them for breakfast. Why not again?

Why not indeed? I had a field, and I could do what I liked with it. Bears could be kept in it. Holes could be dug in it. It could be covered with sand, while one pretended to be at the sea-side. I did not want to do any of these things. I wanted to grow mushrooms. I went indoors and looked them up in the Encyclopædia.

The Encyclopædia said 'see Agaricus'. I saw

43

Agaricus, and was rather pained by the squalid atmosphere in which mushrooms appeared to flourish. There were all sorts of references to fresh horse droppings, stained straw, and decayed top-spit loam. Moreover, when one came to the mushrooms themselves, there was no reference to seeds or cuttings, but only to 'spawn'.

Spawn? Spawn sounded very obscene. If one started throwing spawn about, anything might happen. Perhaps the Encyclopædia was wrong? I turned to Sutton's catalogue. Here again was the hated word, and underneath it a picture of a mushroom bed so prolific that it looked like a crowd scene in one of Rex Ingram's mammoth pictures. There was also a pretty little illustration of Amateur's Mushroom spawn, in which the mushrooms looked a little smaller, modester, and generally less aggressive. So I ordered a lot of Amateur's spawn. I also ordered a cartload of manure and quantities of nitrate of soda and sulphate of ammonia. These were recommended as tonics.

The encyclopædia said you had to plant them — or rather 'it' — in the middle of June. I did the planting on June 15th, all over the field. It was a stormy day, and the wind was in the north — if that interests anybody.

On June 16th, I made a thorough examination of the places where we had planted 'it'. Nothing had happened. Feeling slightly hysterical at the delay, like an anxious father, I sped into Peterborough and bought a lot of little flags at Woolworth's. I chose flags of all the nations, and tore back home again.

44

There was still no sign of any mushroom. With a heavy heart I made the tour of the field, sticking in the flags. The vicar asked me, that evening, if I was going to have a fête. I gave him a mirthless smile, and said 'I hope so.'

That was on June 16th. By August 16th all the flags had blown down, or had been eaten by rabbits, or stolen by the village boys. But not a mushroom had appeared. The field of my neighbour, who had done nothing to deserve it, was white with mushrooms. They sprang up overnight, and stared at me with mocking faces.

I tried to console myself by the thought that they might be only toadstools, but even this illusion was taken from me, for my housekeeper began to pick them and give them to me for breakfast. They were disgustingly good.

Then, one day, an astonishing thing happened. I was walking through the kitchen garden when I saw a white spot on the vegetable marrow bed. It was a mushroom! Closer inspection revealed that it was surrounded by literally hundreds of mushrooms. I rushed to the house, and breathlessly spread the news. S. — my gardener — came, with maddening slowness and deliberation, to the scene of action. 'Oh yes,' he said. 'When you were putting 'em in the field, I just crumbled up a brick of spawn and shoved it in here for luck.'

'You did *what?*'

He repeated the information. I could not disguise my fury. Here he was, talking about 'just crumbling

45

up' one brick and 'shoving' it in. Whereas I had not 'just crumbled up' my spawn. With infinite reverence I had divided the particles, not of one brick but of hundreds. Encyclopædia in hand, I had covered myself with manure, and rushed about with cans of water. I had sprinkled powerful tonics on my spawn, breathed prayers over it and decorated it with flags. And not one mushroom appeared.

The crowning insult came a week later. I had just arrived, and had shunted my car into the makeshift garage, which has a brick floor that is usually covered with oil and petrol. As I stepped out of the car I saw a large white patch in the corner. With a glazed eye, I approached it. Mushrooms! Half a dozen . . . of superb size and quality, pushing up through the bricks, the oil and the dust.

S. arrived to take my bag. Speechless, I pointed with a trembling finger to the corner. He smiled sweetly. 'That's where I put the bag the spawn came in,' he said. 'Rummy things, mushrooms. You can't keep 'em down.'

Personally, I now prefer prawns.

§ v

The mushrooms were only one example of a great many early blunders. You see, I was still under the spell of seed catalogues. I would gaze with rapturous eyes at the photographs of some duke's garden in the south, over which generations of slaves had toiled, into whose rich soil coffers of gold had been spilt,

46

and I would imagine that the same purple miracles, the same riotous abundance could be achieved in my own few yards of newly conquered clay.

I wanted my garden to bloom like the gardens of the Arabian nights. When my father, who comes from a long line of gentlemen farmers, adjusted his eyeglass, glared at the kitchen garden, told me that the soil would need to be turned in the autumn so that the frost could get into it, and that after the frost had got in, we could plant cabbages, I said that I did not want cabbages. I wanted gourds.

'Gourds?' he said. 'What the devil for?'

'I want gourds,' I repeated. 'I can't tell you why I want gourds because you are my father and you would not understand. But I want them, and it is my garden.'

I also wanted sweet corn. I also wanted Couve Tronchuda, principally because of its name. It sounded like a peculiar edition of Tallulah Bankhead. But principally I wanted gourds.

The gourds had large seeds like dry beans and I planted them in all sorts of unexpected places, with the idea that they would pop out from the darkness, like faces. I hoped that people would be terrified of them, so I decided to scratch eyes and mouths on them when they came up. But they never came up. Only one appeared, looking like a rather rude fungus, and it was promptly eaten by a slug. However the Couve Tronchuda flourished, and I wish that it had not done because it not only sounded like a Spanish dancer but tasted like one . . . very sweet and stringy. The sweet corn also did remarkably well, but one gets very messy eating it, and it is really much nicer in tins.

It was not till I experimented with seeds plucked straight from a growing plant that I had my first success . . . the first thrill of *creation* . . . the first taste of blood. This, surely, must be akin to the pride of paternity . . . indeed, many soured bachelors would wager that it must be almost as wonderful to see the first tiny crinkled leaves of one's first plant as to see the tiny crinkled face of one's first child.

In both cases, it is to be supposed, the predominant emotion is incredulity. 'Was *I* really responsible for this?' asks the young father, as he holds the child in his arms . . . Sometimes he is not entirely convinced that the answer is in the affirmative.

§ v i

My first experiment was with a lupin which flowered unexpectedly in the garden three months after my arrival. When the flowers were over, the pods split open, revealing seeds, and in a mad moment I decided to plant these seeds. 'This is mad,' I said to myself as I tipped out the small black pellets. 'Quite mad. Do you seriously think they will come up, for you? Do you honestly imagine that this creative miracle is actually going to occur?'

I really did ask these questions, simply because seeds that had failed to receive the baptism of a penny or sixpenny packet seemed, somehow, not quite authentic. Of course, the conscious mind proclaimed

48

that all seeds had to come, originally, from flowers, and that therefore these hot, ripe lupin seeds, plucked straight from a healthy plant, had as much chance of success as any that could be bought at a shop, even at Woolworth's. But the subconscious mind demanded the packet. It wanted to see the beautiful blurred picture on the cover. It wanted to read that they formed 'gigantic spikes of dazzling blue flowers,' and other fearful lies like that.

The conscious mind won. I said to myself 'you are being idiotic. This stalk, in front of you, was once a lupin. The horrid things sticking out all over it are, without question, pods. Inside the pods are small black pellets which are not beads nor eggs nor sweets, but seeds. The obvious course is to go back to Nature, seize some seeds, and put them in the softest, sweetest, most luxurious earth you can find. It would not be surprising if quantities of large aspidistras instantly appear, put out their tongues, and make fearful smells. On the other hand, it would not be surprising if the seeds actually came up as lupins.'

The seeds did come up, as lupins, and it *was* extremely surprising. The surprise lingers to this day. I have just been for a walk in the garden – it is late June – and the seeds that I sowed some time ago are now grown to a whole border of plants, trembling into flower. The sub-conscious mind still cannot believe it. I suppose that it is experiencing the wonder and humiliation of all men who have assisted, in their meagre way, in creating something.

That is why I dragged in the subject of paternity.

If it is possible to gain this exultation, this true and lasting delight from the seed of a cold blue flower, what might not be the frenzy were one to sow one's own seed, to have a son? Ah — but it isn't as simple as that! Sons are not as easy to grow as lupins. Apart from the fact that they frequently turn out to be daughters, you cannot count on their being true to type. The seed of a blue lupin will usually produce a blue lupin. But the seed of a blue-eyed man may produce a brown-eyed bore . . . especially if his wife has a taste for gigolos.

Well, you have read so far, and you are probably saying to yourself that this is all a vague muddle, with far too much irrelevant personal detail, and far too little about the garden itself. 'We can learn nothing from this' you will say.

Please do not throw down the book just yet. For after a very few more pages you *will* learn something. I promise you that. If not, you can go and ask the bookseller for your money back.

CHAPTER IV

MID-WINTER MADNESS

§ 1

WE are now in the depths of winter . . . my first winter at the cottage . . . and the first winter when I went mad.

The average gardener, in the cold dark days of December and January, sits by his fire, turning over the pages of seed catalogues, wondering what he shall sow for the spring. If he goes out in his garden at all it is only for the sake of exercise. He puts on a coat, stamps up and down the frozen paths, hardly deigns to glance at the black empty beds, turns in again. Perhaps, before returning to his fireside, he may go and look into a dark cupboard to see if the hyacinths, in fibre, are beginning to sprout. But that represents the sum total of his activity.

I wrote above that, on this first winter, I went mad. For I suddenly said to myself 'I WILL HAVE FLOWERS IN MY GARDEN IN WINTER.' And by flowers I meant real flowers, not merely a few sprays of frozen periwinkle, and an occasional blackened Christmas rose. Everybody to whom I spoke said that this desire was insane, and I suppose 'everybody' ought to have been right. Yet, everybody was wrong. For my dream has come true.

Now, one more moment of self-revelation and we

51

can really begin. I *must* explain my love of winter flowers, in order that the charge of insanity may be refuted.

And yet it is so strong and so persistent — this love — that I sometimes call a halt, and ask myself if it may not be, at least, a little morbid. For there are curious visions that come to me, on blazing summer days, when the garden is packed with blossom like a basket. In an instant, I seem to see the garden bare . . . the crimsons and the purples are wiped out, the sky is drained of its blue, and the trees stand stark and melancholy against a sky that is the colour of ashes. It is then that I see, in some distant corner, the faint, sad glimmer of the winter jasmine . . . like a match that flickers in the dark . . . and at my feet a pale and lonely Christmas rose. And I kneel down quickly, as though I would shelter this brave flower from the keen wind . . . only to realize with a start, that I am kneeling in the sunshine, that there is no flower there, only a few green leaves . . . and overhead, the burning sun.

I wonder why. And yet, perhaps I know. For this passion for winter flowers has its roots deep, deep within me. I have a horror of endings, of farewells, of every sort of death. The inevitable curve of Nature, which rises so gallantly and falls so ignominiously, is to me a loathsome shape. I want the curve to rise perpetually. I want the rocket, which is life, to soar to measureless heights. I shudder at its fall, and gain no consolation that, in falling, it breaks into trembling stars of acid green and liquid gold. I can hear only the thump of the stick in some sordid back yard. The silly thump of a silly stick. The end of life. What does it matter that a moment ago the tent of night was spangled with green and gold? It is gone, now. The colour is but gas . . . a feeble poison, dissipated. Only the stick remains.

I believe that my love for winter flowers has its secret in this neurosis . . . if one may dignify the condition by such a word. I want my garden to *go on*. I cannot bear to think of it as a place that may be tenanted only in the easy months. I will not have it draped with Nature's dust sheets.

That is why I waged this battle for winter flowers. Make no mistake about it. It *is* a battle. There is the clash of drama about it. People think that the gardener is a placid man, who chews a perpetual cud . . . a man whose mind moves slowly, like an expanding leaf, whose spirit is as calm as the earth's breath, whose eyes are as bright as the morning dew. Such ideas are very wide of the mark. A gardener . . . if he is like many gardeners I know . . . is a wild and highly-strung creature, whose mind trembles like the aspen and is warped by sudden frosts and scarred by strange winds. His spirit is as tenuous as the mists that hang, like ghosts, about the winter orchards, and in his eyes one can see the shadows of clouds on black and distant hills.

§ II

As soon as I had decided that I was going to specialize in winter flowers, I began to study the catalogues. Very crudely, at first. I used to turn to the lists of chrysanthemums, and choose the latest flowering varieties, forgetting that they needed the protection of glass. Then I would get hold of the bulb lists, and choose the earliest flowering bulbs . . . little knowing that the average bulb merchant was a master of deceit, and gaily advertised his wares as blooming in January when, in fact, they would not deign to thrust their green caps through the earth until the beginning of March. I knew all about the winter jasmine of course, and I ordered a dozen of these. Also a quantity of clumps of Christmas roses. There my knowledge of winter flowers stopped. And so I began to write to various nurseries, asking them what they could recommend.

The nurseries could recommend winter jasmine and Christmas roses. When they had made these two brilliant suggestions, their ingenuity appeared to be exhausted. The correspondence invariably trailed off into vague generalities. When I wrote to them that there must surely be *something* besides winter jasmine and Christmas roses, they replied with dark hints, saying that of course there *were* things, but it was doubtful whether they would 'do,' and perhaps it might be as well to meet 'our Mr. Wilkins'. But I did not desire to meet their Mr. Wilkins. I wanted to be told about winter flowers.

Of course, I had written to the wrong nurseries. There *are* places which specialize in winter flowers, but I did not know about them.

For this reason my garden, on its first winter, was as

barren as ever. A few snowdrops, of the feeblest variety, thinly planted. One or two sprays of jasmine. Not a solitary Christmas rose.

§III

It was during that first barren January that my passion for winter flowers developed into an obsession. I felt that somewhere somebody was waiting to tell me something. But who? And where? And what? I threw the catalogues into the fire, and watched their false pages curling into smoke. They were deceivers, those catalogues. I went back to London.

It was in such a state of depression that I strolled, one bleak January morning, into Messrs. Hatchard's bookshop at 187 Piccadilly. I was after a copy of George Moore's *Confessions of a Young Man*, for my own copy was almost worn out, so passionately had it been fondled. I walked into the shop, muttered something about 'looking for a book', and went to the shelves where Moore lay, in lofty seclusion.

But as I looked up, I saw that I had come to the wrong section. The books in front of me were all about gardening. They did not seem to be very attractive. They were mostly in wrappers which showed women in obsolete hats standing with guilty expressions by the side of immense hollyhocks. They had terrible titles too . . . like 'Romps in the Rockery' and 'A Garden of Memorie'. I was about to pass on when suddenly I saw, right by my hand, a book with a title that made me catch my breath in excitement.

It was called *Winter Blossoms from the Outdoor Garden,* by A. W. Darnell.

Gingerly I stretched out my hand to take it. Would it vanish into thin air? No. It was real enough. However, as I took it down, I felt that surely there must be some catch somewhere. For months I had been vainly searching the catalogues and the encyclopædias for even a few paragraphs about winter flowers. And here was a whole book devoted to the problem. Was the title a fake? Was it not a garden book at all . . . was it perhaps an awful collection of sentimental short stories? About thin sickly children who grew ivy in slums . . . and all that?

I opened it. And as soon as I read the introduction, my anxiety ceased. Here is what Mr. Darnell says:—

Beyond the Winter Jasmine, Christmas Roses, and Laurustinus, but few of the winter blossoming plants described in the following pages are to be seen outdoors in the average gardens of Great Britain. In the hope that lovers of winter blossoms may be induced to grow such subjects more freely, and glean some of the pleasure that has been his, the author has compiled the following pages from voluminous notes made over a period of many years. These observations have taught him that given shelter, a warm soil, and a normal season, the smallest suburban garden may be made to yield sheaves of beautiful blossoms for table and room decoration throughout our winter months.

The commoner inhabitants of the amateur's garden such as: Roses, Chrysanthemums, Michaelmas Daisies, Primroses,

56

Violets, etc., that frequently muster sufficient precocity or belatedness to supply a few blossoms on Christmas Day in mild seasons, have not been included, the space being allotted to less well-known plants. Care has been taken to include only those plants which may be expected to give their blossoms during the months specified on the title-page of the book; they have, with but few exceptions, been repeatedly observed by the author in blossom year after year during that period.

This was so absolutely the book that I had been seeking that I bought it at once, and rushed out of the shop, forgetting all about George Moore.

§IV

Let me observe, without delay, that I do not know Mr. Darnell, nor anything about him. I would like to know him very much indeed, but I have not that honour. I have not even written to him. I only say this in order to relieve your suspicions that we are in some awful league together. He has not scratched my back, nor have I scratched his. Nor do I expect to, though I should like to *stroke* his back, very gently and with a decently controlled ecstasy, for the pleasure and instruction he has given me.

In this book (which is published by L. Reeve and Co. Ltd., Bank Street, Ashford, Kent), you will find nearly everything about winter flowers that is known to modern man. Its full title is: —

DOWN THE GARDEN PATH

A DESCRIPTIVE LIST OF EXOTIC
TREES, SHRUBS AND HERBACEOUS PLANTS
THAT FLOWER IN THE OUTDOOR GARDEN IN
THE BRITISH ISLES
DURING THE MONTHS OF DECEMBER, JANUARY AND
FEBRUARY.

(Presumably, these trees, shrubs and herbaceous plants will, with few exceptions, flower equally well in most North American districts. It would be interesting to know.)

I said, a moment ago, that Mr. Darnell and I were not engaged in any unholy conspiracy together. I would reinforce that statement by venturing one or two criticisms of his book.

For instance, on several occasions, he is madly optimistic. Thus, on the very first page, there is a beautiful plate, drawn with his own hand, of the *Acacia Baileyana*, which most of us call mimosa, though the Australians, somewhat unkindly, call it 'wattle'. 'How's that?' you will exclaim. 'Mimosa? Out of doors in the British Isles?' And then you will make that noise which one writes as 'Pshaw!' At least that is the noise which I made, when I thought of those pale powdered tassels vainly endeavouring to withstand the cutting winds of the Midlands . . . stretching their sensitive roots into the cold, sullen clay of Huntingdonshire.

Perhaps this is a little unfair to Mr. Darnell. For if you read the opening phrases of his first section you will perceive that he breathes about the *Acacia*

SPRING

Baileyana an atmosphere of warmth and cosiness which the poor plant, alas, encounters but seldom in these climes. He writes:

In many gardens in Devonshire and Cornwall, in spots sheltered from the north and east by a living wall of evergreen trees, but open to the sun's rays, grand specimens of this glorious tree may be seen in full flower in the month of January . . .

Well, that may be so. But we do not all live in Devonshire and Cornwall. We are not all the possessors of spots sheltered from the north and east. We have not, all of us, a living wall of evergreen trees. We want something more definite than that.

Mr. Darnell, as soon as he gets beyond the awkward letter A, which appears to have unduly exalted him, makes no more impossible demands. He leaves Devonshire and Cornwall. He caters for the Midlands, for the open spaces, for the hard ungrateful soils, for the bitterest and sourest tempers of winter. Yet always his hands are full of flowers . . . and they are real flowers, too, as I have learnt from sweet experience. Sometimes they may not be flamboyant . . . their petals may be nearer to green than to gold . . . their beauty may be shy and timid . . . over their faces they may stretch green leaves to shield them from the wind, or they may droop diffidently to the kindly earth, afraid to rear their heads too high. But they are flowers, all the same. And they flower as Mr. Darnell states, in December, January and February. Let us make their acquaintance.

61

§ v

If you are a great expert, with a case of medals from the Horticultural Society on your mantelpiece . . . if you have written treatises on the *Ionopsidium Acaule* (which, by the way, is well worth growing) . . . if you have a huge drooping moustache and a huge drooping head-gardener, then you had better throw this book aside. I am not writing for you. I really have not the least idea for whom I am writing. For the flowers themselves, I expect. For the really simple, absolutely trustworthy winter flowers that may be guaranteed to spangle the garden with blossom whatever the weather, whatever the soil, and whatever the international situation.

First and foremost among these I would place the winter aconite. By some extraordinary oversight Mr. Darnell does not mention it at all, which is the only serious criticism I have to make about his book.

The winter aconite is included in nearly every bulb catalogue. That is about all the publicity this brave and radiant blossom has ever gained. It is just 'included'. It is never starred, as it should be. It is given a tiny paragraph, down at the bottom of the page, with a curt note saying that it is 'one of the first spring flowers. Effective in borders. Fifty shillings a thousand.'

It is *not* 'one of the first spring flowers.' It is a midwinter flower. It is not 'effective'. It is dazzling. And, from my experience, it would come up if you planted it on an iceberg.

MID-WINTER MADNESS

I am sorry to get so hot about the winter aconite, but I hate to see these lovely things neglected. I hate to think of all the bare gloomy spaces in English and American gardens, in mid-January, when they might all be made as gay as a buttercup field.

A buttercup field in mid-January! That is what the aconites will do for you, if you buy enough of them. For the aconite is like a large, brilliant buttercup with a green ruff round its neck, and nothing will stop it from flowering. Its brave gold is untarnished by rain, by snow, by the fiercest degrees of frost. I once planted some aconites in low ground under trees. Shortly after Christmas the ground was flooded. Then came the frost, and a thick sheet of ice covered the whole area. Yet the aconites pushed their way through the earth, expanded their blossoms, and gleamed beneath the ice, like a Victorian posy under a glass case.

They are particularly lovely when there are a few inches of snow on the ground. Their stems are just tall enough to lift the blossoms above the white coverlet. The effect is of gold-spangled satin. But they are lovely too on the mild days, for then they open very wide, and one sees how essentially innocent and childlike they are, which makes their courage and endurance all the more remarkable.

You cannot have too many aconites. They cost, as I said before, about fifty shillings a thousand. A thousand will make a brave splash of colour, which lasts a month. If you can afford ten thousand, you are mad not to buy them. There are so many exciting places you can put them . . . in the hollow of a felled tree, by the border of a pond, in a circle round a statue, or immediately under your window, so that you can press your nose against the glass, when it is too cold to go out, and stare at them, and remember that spring is on its way.

§ VI

After the aconites, I place, in order of excitement, the *Chimonanthus fragrans*, which is better known by its charming name of wintersweet. There is a delightful picture of it in Mr. Darnell's book, showing a creamy yellow flower, prettily striped with red. This picture does not lie. As Mr. Darnell says 'From a well-established specimen, planted against a warm wall, we may expect to gather long sprays of its pretty highly fragrant flowers in the very depth of winter with absolute certainty.'

My plants . . . I have a dozen of them . . . have only been 'established' for three years, and they have not the shelter of a warm wall . . . only a thin wooden fence protects them. Yet, last year, the spare brown branches were lavishly starred with blossom, soon after Christmas. If they were cut in bud, they lasted . . . with the discreet assistance of a tablet of aspirin . . . nearly a month. Their perfume was as sweet and delicate as anything you could desire.

Do not forget the importance of picking many winter flowers in bud. It is a secret which brings astonishing rewards. Most people, for example, do not realize how exquisite the common *jasminum nudi-florum* can be, for indoor decoration, if it is properly treated. They see it on their suburban porches, tattered and brown and windswept, with a lot of tiresome twigs surrounding the flowers, and they hardly ever bother to cut it and give it shelter.

Yet, if you go out, and run your fingers over the shrub, you will find quantities of young branches, bearing an abundance of buds. Some of these buds may be barely formed . . . they may show you only a gleam of yellow, with a reddish-brown tip. They may be cluttered up with a lot of dead wood. Be brave! Slice off those branches. Carry them indoors. Trim off the dead wood. Place the result in water. Leave them for a week in a dark, warm cupboard. When you return you will find that the jasmine has broken into the gayest blossom . . . a bright, sturdy array of blossom that lasts, literally for weeks. Then, as you tuck some asparagus fern from the greenhouse into the vase, and transport it proudly to your desk, you will feel inclined to ask the question 'Who said that it was cruel to cut flowers? When these are as happy as primroses in a sheltered corner?' And, one might add, as expensive-looking as any spray of orchids.

§ VII

And now, quickly, to the next winter flower, the witch-hazel. (I refer to the *Hamamelis mollis*, by far the most vigorous variety.)

It is a melancholy thought that the millions of tired shop-girls who wearily smear their faces with watered extracts of this enchanting plant, every night, should know so little about it. A very melancholy thought indeed. For the shop girls, as they dab on to their parched skins its healing essences, are not reflecting upon the true, sweet source from which the healing comes. No. They are only recalling that the cold cream, in which the magic lurks, is also being applied by a quantity of Mrs. Vanderbilts and Lady Dianas.

It would be better if there could dance, before their tired eyes, the impudent, shining sequins of the *Hamamelis mollis.* The feathery, spidery, yellow exuberance of this darling plant! For was there ever such bravery, such delicious effrontery, as is displayed, on many quiet walls throughout England, by the witch-hazel in mid-winter? Oh, it is much to be praised, infinitely to be exalted, this strong and delicate flower! There is something theatrical about it. To discover it, on a dark day, glistening epigrammatically in a forsaken world, magnificently pert and yellow, is so inspiring that one's hands automatically begin to clap, as though one were applauding a witty actress who was tossing her pretty head at a damned difficult situation.

I shall never forget the thrill I had when I saw my first witch-hazel in bloom. It was a bitter day in early February, and I arrived at the cottage just as it was getting dark. I was tired and depressed. Work was going badly. There was a slump on Wall Street, a pain in my leg, and a fierce north-east wind. I will not pretend that all these mental and physical ills were completely cured by the witch-hazel. But at least, it made me forget them until the next morning.

I was 'making the tour' as usual, and for once in a way I thought I would cut it short. The witch-hazel was situated at the farthest end of the orchard wall. It was really hardly worth while going to look at it, on a night like this. After all, I had watched it for weeks, and there had never been a sign of life. The buds remained like cloves, apparently sealed with a seal that would never break until spring.

Then I said to myself 'I must not get into bad habits. If I cut the tour short now, I shall always be cutting it short. A spell will be broken. Things will never be the same again. I shall go to the farthest corner of the orchard wall, see the witch-hazel, curse its barren twigs, and go in to have a drink.'

I went. And there, in the gathering darkness, with the high, strange wind roaring through the great elm branches above me, I saw that the twigs of the witch hazel had broken into golden stars.

It was a miracle. Surely there is no need to emphasize that. It was akin to the barren fig tree. It was . . . but we must curb our excitement. There are more winter flowers, waiting round the corner.

CHAPTER V

MORE WINTER FLOWERS

§ I

EVEN if you invested only in the winter aconite, the wintersweet and the witch-hazel, you would have plenty of flowers in the middle of January. All of them, however, would be yellow flowers. So let us introduce some pinks and blues.

The pinks you may obtain, with absolute certainty, from several heathers, though the *erica carnea* is much the hardiest and most impudent. You can have whole months of thrills from the *erica carnea*. It begins to drop hints of what it is proposing to do as early as September, but the hints are so quiet and discreet that one pays small attention to them. Then, as the autumn progresses, the little greeny-white buds swell slightly, and towards the beginning of December there is an authentic tinge of pink in them. This tinge deepens quickly, until at last, round about Christmas time, the bells flush to a lovely rose colour. And this colour is maintained until spring is well on its way.

They are adorable, these clumps of winter heather. Actually they seem to welcome the snow, for it enhances their sweet complexions. They demand no care, they crave no shelter. Their one request is that you should plant them in good, peaty loam. Plenty of it. Not merely a little top dressing over a hard bed of clay. If you do this for them, they will do the rest themselves. I think that it is fun to plant them at the extreme end of the garden, as far from the house as possible, in order that you may have an excuse to make long expeditions, and be able to see their welcome colour gleaming from afar.

There are several other *ericas*, with which you might well experiment. But the *erica carnea* is the only variety which I can heartily recommend from personal experience.

§ 11

Now for the blues. To find blue flowers, growing out of doors, in the depths of winter, without any artificial shelter at all, would surprise most people as much as if they suddenly found a huge dodo sitting in the bath, rolling its eyes at them, and saying 'Hoosh!' Yet . . . it can be done.

If you want to begin with something that is quite foolproof, you cannot do better than invest in a few roots of *Petasites fragrans* which has the pretty English name of winter heliotrope. Some people sneer at the winter heliotrope. They say the flower is dingy, and that the roots have abominable habits, being inclined to spread indiscriminately into the garden next door. The people next door should be very grateful if the roots *do* spread into their garden. For the flower is not dingy at all . . . it is a little pale and humble . . . that is all. Besides, one does not grow the winter heliotrope for its beauty of form. One grows it for its beauty of scent. It has a most exquisite fragrance. If you cut it and carry it indoors it will scent a whole room. I always put a few flowers in my winter bunches for this reason alone.

However, there are far finer blues, far lovelier blossoms than the winter heliotrope, which is best regarded as a disembodied perfume.

The best of all is the *Iris stylosa*, (or the *Iris ungincularis*, if you are feeling high hat). It is a real sky blue . . . not the deep blue of summer, but the brilliant paler blue of a frosty January day. The lower petals have gold patches in their centres, spotted with purple. If you want a finer flower than this in winter, you had better go and lock yourself up in your greenhouse and sing hymns.

However . . . the *Iris stylosa* has peculiar habits. It takes a long time to decide whether it is going to like you or not. It is rather like a temperamental prima donna. I speak as a veteran of three years experience, which is the average period required for the *Iris stylosa* to settle down. Here is the record of my own plants: —

First year. Twenty clumps planted in June. Two were dead by October. The rest survived but did not produce a single flower.

Second year. Suddenly, in the middle of May, three plants put out large blue tongues at me, in the shape of fine and authentic flowers. They were entirely out of order in flowering at this time. They seemed to be saying 'So you thought you were only going to allow us out in winter, did you? This'll learn you!'

Three more plants died that winter. In January two very feeble blossoms appeared.

Third year. All through the spring and summer the remaining fifteen plants put on a prodigious amount of leaf. By this time I had given up much hope of ever getting any flowers from them. However, I took a hint from a friend who told me that they liked a coarse soil. and that I had been feeding them too well. So I sprinkled a lot of gravel over the roots, which seemed the best way of coarsening the soil, and also helped to drain it. Whether they were already 'established', without the gravel's assistance, I do not know. In any case, the first bloom appeared at the beginning of December, and by Christmas day all the plants were flowering. Some of the stems were a good nine inches high and nearly all the flowers were fine and brilliantly coloured.

Do not, therefore, be rude or unkind to your *Iris stylosa* if, at first, it does not appear to be trying.

§ III

However, even the *Iris stylosa* is beaten for loveliness of colour by the glowing purply blue of the *crocus imperati*. Most people regard a crocus as a spring flower . . . if it were ever to come up before March they would think that something very odd was happening, and would go round muttering about sun-spots, or observing that one never knew what to expect, now that the atmosphere was so disturbed by all this radio.

Well, certain crocuses *like* coming up in January and February, and the radio and the sun-spots have nothing whatever to do with it. You may say 'what does it matter whether they come up in January or in March, provided they do come up?' However if you were capable of asking that question you would not be reading me at all, for unless you long to defeat winter, to make your gardening year an *endless* chain of blossom, this would all be a sorry bore for you.

To return to the *crocus imperati*. You will not find it in the average bulb catalogue, though some of the bigger firms list it. However, even when they do condescend to mention it, they hide it away, as though it were in disgrace, and they seem to have no fixed idea about its price. Some merchants will charge you as much for a dozen as for a hundred, so it behoves you to make adequate enquiries before you buy it. However, buy it you must. For nothing can be lovelier than its purple centres with their striped lilac exteriors. It comes up without fail in January, and even when the sky is a dirty frozen grey it opens its bland and innocent blossoms, like a child that does not understand the meaning of danger.

There are many other crocuses . . . (Mr. Darnell mentions over a hundred) . . . but the few that I have tried have proved difficult and recalcitrant, and it is almost impossible to obtain them at a reasonable price. The only one with which I had any success was the *crocus sieberi*. But they were neither so early nor so pretty as the *imperati*. They did not come out till the middle of February, and most of them were white.

§ I V

We are almost at the end of our blues — for I am not writing for specialists nor millionaires, and it would take too long to describe all the little plants which are scattered throughout my garden in sheltered corners. I am assuming that you have only a little money and a sullen soil and that you do not live at Cornwall or Charleston, but near Manchester or Minnesota. If you do live near either of these places, it is difficult to see how you can possibly exist without the assistance of the *Daphne mezereum*.

This plant is not really a blue at all . . . it is a pinkish-purple. And when you have once seen it in flower, you will not wish it to be any other colour. However, you will not see it in flower at all unless you take a deep breath and learn this by heart:

'*The* Daphne mezereum *loves its roots in the shade and its head in the sun. The secret of its successful cultivation is a cool root run, deep and moist, but well drained, for it is very short lived in hot dry soils.*'

This is bitterly true. I had six *Daphnes* and only one has survived, because this was the only one which was properly planted. The soil was dug very deep, and a protecting arm of evergreen honeysuckle shaded the roots. The branches were sheltered by a western wall. Against this wall, in the second year, the blossoms shone divinely. They began to come out at the end of January and by the middle of February the bare stems were thickly spangled with the flowers, which smelt as sweet as freesias.

But if we are in search of scent . . . nothing can equal the *lonicera fragrantissima*. Being translated, this is honeysuckle. It is strange that in this England of ours we should always think of honeysuckle as linked with harvest, and summer skies, and sultry lanes through which the towering hay-wagons lumber. Honeysuckle makes most people recall lemonade, and country girls in bonnets, and parched grass and all the rest of it. However, I am perverse, so it makes me think of icicles. For there were long icicles dripping from the rain-gutters on the sparkling January morning when I first found my winter honeysuckle in flower. The drops fell, like truant diamonds, from the icicles on to the frozen, creamy petals. Yet, the flower was not deterred. It shook off the drops, and continued to emit its fantastic sweetness. By the time the sun was high, the scent was quite overpowering.

The flowers are not, of course, as large as those of the summer honeysuckle. I cannot talk learnedly about corollas, lips, lobes, and axils. I can only say that the blooms are extremely pretty, and look as if they had been quarrelling, for they are usually placed back to back. As far as I know they are not fastidious about soil. I merely put mine into the common clay, which had been roughly treated with a little sand and loam.

The flowers last for a fortnight if you cut them in the bud. And they send out such a perpetual stream of fragrance that you will long to rush about the house waving scarves and doing spring songs, protruding your lips and breathing with suspicious violence.

§ v

Are you bored?

Indeed I hope not. For the flowers' sake, not for my own. At the risk of out-winnying the poo, it must be admitted that I always think flowers know what you are saying about them. If I see a scraggly lupin, I like to pass well out of its hearing before delivering any adverse comments on it. For how do we know what tortures it may be suffering? It surely can be no more pleasant for a lupin to have to appear with tarnished petals than for a woman to be forced to walk about with a spotty face. One does not say 'Oh look at that awful girl covered with pimples!' Why then, should one stand over flowers and hurl insults at them? Besides, the flowers' condition may be all your own fault, which cannot be said of the girl's complexion, unless she is a particular friend of yours and you have been keeping her up too late at nights.

I can therefore only hope that some of my love for winter flowers has been transmitted to these pages. If not, it is a bad look-out for you. We have not done with them yet.

I am writing a floral autobiography, so I am con-

75

fining myself strictly to the flowers that I have grown myself. Moreover, I promise to include only those which can be absolutely guaranteed to come up in mid-winter, with a minimum of shelter and care.

One of these is the *corylopsis spicata*. This is a lovely bush covered with little yellow bouquets that smell exactly like cowslips. One is bound to admit that if the winter is very severe, the flowers will not appear before March. However, in a fairly mild season, they will come out at the end of January. The *corylopsis spicata* revels in sand around its roots. I poured a whole sack-full round mine, with the happiest result. The average nurseryman, when asked for the *corylopsis*, will flinch, and look the other way, as though you had made a highly criminal suggestion to him. However, if you persevere, he will eventually talk sense, and will 'procure' one, even if he has not got it in stock.

On no account must you neglect the *Sternbergea lutea*. This is an early winter flower, as opposed to most of the others I have mentioned, i.e. it flowers from the end of October until Christmas.

People call it the winter daffodil, but it is really much more like a large and peculiarly brilliant crocus. For this reason it is best planted in the grass, near the house, if possible. But you should see that it is not placed in the drip of the trees, because though its petals may be frozen with impunity, and though it will stand any amount of wind . . . (in which it differs strangely from the ordinary crocus) . . . it hates being dribbled upon.

Because I have not space to tell of many more winter flowers please do not assume that I have mentioned even a quarter of those which you may grow with an assurance of delight. There are, for example, quantities of saxifrages which may be counted upon to produce their tiny starred blossoms throughout the darkest, most shivering days. Of these I can personally recommend the *Saxifraga ciliata*, which is rather like a lovely white cowslip. With any luck you will be able to pick it on New Year's Day. It will offer you the prettiest thanks if you cover it with a sheet of glass when the weather is exceptionally rough.

Nor can I pass on without mentioning the *Forsythia intermedia*, a true winter shrub if ever there was one, for even in London its bare branches are covered with golden-yellow blossoms in mid-February, while I have had it out, against a sheltered wall, before the end of January.

Nor again, the *cyclamen coum*, nor the *berberis japonica* . . . but if I go on like this, there will be no end. I must therefore content myself by a few very pedestrian observations on two of the commonest winter flowers of all, the Christmas rose and the snowdrop. It is very seldom that one sees either of these growing in anything like their proper size or abundance in English gardens.

The average Christmas rose is a sickly, squalid-looking thing. Half its petals are black. The stalk is only about an inch high. It looks as if it had a fearful cold in the head. Nobody could possibly go into raptures about it.

Yet, I have grown Christmas roses as white as lilies, with stalks a foot long. Christmas roses that were so fair that they were like some radiant gardenia. I once had a bowl of such fine specimens that people thought they were orchids.

The secret is very simple. Firstly, you must grow them in deep shade. Then they will be forced to produce stalks. Put them in a wood, or shrubbery, or under a thick evergreen. Secondly, you must protect them with a cloche . . . i.e. a little tent of glass, which you can buy from any garden shop. Some people think this is cheating, but if you could only see the result, you would risk the damage to your soul.

Now about the snowdrops. Most people are abysmally ignorant about snowdrops. They buy feeble little bulbs that come up late and never reach a decent size. In January, when the ground outside my window is white with snowdrops almost as large as cyclamen, I have often opened my newspaper to read a letter from some benighted woman saying that she picked three snowdrops from a sheltered position in her Devonshire garden, and isn't it wonderful? It is. It is wonderful that she and the editor should be so ignorant.

If you want huge snowdrops, of a white that dazzles and of a shape that is perfection, and if you want to have them very soon after Christmas, there are only two things that you must do, and one thing that you must remember. Firstly, you must buy the variety *Galanthus elwesii*. It is, of course, a more expensive bulb, but you would be expensive too, if you looked like that. Secondly, you must plant it at least six inches deep. I have not the vaguest idea why, but you must. And the thing you have to remember is that they will not be so large in succeeding years as they are in their first year. They will be large, but not gigantic. Nor would you trouble to be gigantic, if you had made so superb a début. You see, I will not hear a word spoken against my snowdrops.

They are heavenly, when they are out, and set in a glass bowl, so that their fresh green stalks are seen with the water-bubbles glistening around them.

If you want snowdrops for massing under trees, there are all sorts of cheap varieties. However, they are at least six weeks later than the *elwesii*, and I myself will have none of them. I shall probably go bankrupt, with my tastes. But I would rather be made bankrupt by a bulb merchant than by a chorus girl.

CHAPTER VI

GARDEN FRIENDS

§ I

I SEEM to have broken into technicalities rather earlier than I intended. However it was the fault of the winter flowers, which lured me on with their cold blossoms, like ice-maidens.

We must return to the story of the slow and painful transformation of a wilderness into a garden. We must tell how the rock garden was made, how the little wood came to be planted, how the greenhouse was changed from a sort of glorified meat-safe into a flowery, perfumed place of magic. The very thought of these things makes me want to bounce up and down on my chair and blow out my cheeks with pleasure.

However, if we are to be honest, it must be admitted that these achievements, which will shortly be described, were not all my own work. To some of them I was inspired, to some goaded. Constantly, in the background, there flitted friends and relations, and I think that it is only fair to pay tribute where it is due. (Incidentally, I hope that I may be able to wipe off a few old scores.)

Let us therefore meet some of these gardening friends.

A garden can make or mar a friendship. It brings out all sorts of hidden virtues and unsuspected vices.

GARDEN FRIENDS

By no means all of my friends are gardeners and I never say to people 'would you like to look at the garden?' because any lover of gardens, even if he sees only a lawn and a solitary herbaceous border, will ask to see it himself.

But one's friends who *are* gardeners . . . how a garden shows them up! It is as though a curious light were reflected from the petals of the flowers — a light in which the emotions are sharply revealed. I saw this light most clearly on the face of a middle-aged lady whom I will call Miss Hazlitt, and I believe I am not exaggerating if I say that it was divine.

She was the first woman who ever stayed with me in my cottage.

§ 11

She was lying in Charing Cross hospital when I saw her. It had been twelve years since we met, and I fear that I had done little to deserve that she should remember me. Perhaps my tardiness as a correspondent was partly due to a certain embarrassment.

Religious people trouble me . . . possibly because they have a gift which I cannot find, nor buy, nor cultivate. But it was impossible to be irritated by Miss Hazlitt, even when she expounded the doctrine of Faith Without Works, in her sweet, country voice. 'If you would only have *faith*!' she would cry. Once, in a rare exasperation (more at myself than at her) I said to her 'you might as well say "if I would only have red hair, or a tenor voice, or blue eyes" . . . you either have these things or you don't . . . you either believe or disbelieve.' She only shook her head, and smiled, and put her hand on mine. I could not resent this. One does not resent the actions of a saint.

Only a saint could have borne without resentment the grotesque and squalid course of events which had led her to Charing Cross hospital. She had suffered for years from neuritis in her right arm. This had made it difficult for her to play games with the children whom she was teaching. Her employers had shaken their heads, dropped hints that perhaps she was growing a little old . . . She was very sensitive, and when the local doctor told her that the neuritis was caused by her teeth, which should all be extracted, she gave notice, scraped a little money together, and had the teeth out.

At least, she thought that she had her teeth out. Actually, the dentist was criminally incompetent, and left many of the roots in. She grew worse. Her money was almost gone. After many humiliating vicissitudes she was brought to the hospital and it was here that I found her.

She was lying in a little ward that contained, beside herself, two working women and a Swedish girl who lay with a waxen face, the fumes of ether still about her. Outside, the noise of the traffic roared perpetually and the October rain lashed the panes. Yet, over Miss Hazlitt's bed there seemed to hover an aura of serenity. She was toothless, she wore a rough pink nightdress, her hair was lank, and her face was drawn. She looked happier than I ever hope to look.

I gave her a little bunch of roses, sat down on a hard chair, talked inanely. It was then that I learnt the last blow that had been dealt her. Instead of being out of her agony, she was beginning it. Almost the first words she heard, when she awoke, were: 'Your mouth was in such a bad condition that we could not finish the operation. You will have to have another . . . perhaps two.' This meant that she would not be able to take up the new position which a lucky chance had offered her.

I asked her to come down with me to the cottage, as soon as she was well enough to be moved.

§III

You may call me sentimental, moonstruck, what you will, but I swear that the flowers welcomed her. The date was October 5th, and I copy two notes from my diary: The first was written before she arrived.

'*To-day marks the end of summer time, and indeed the garden is reflecting it too. Early fallen leaves are whirling down the crazy pavements, the grass is a sadder green, and some of the flowers are beginning to have their complexions tarnished.*'

Two nights later, as Miss Hazlitt lay upstairs in bed, I wrote:

'*I never picked a finer, sturdier bunch of roses than to-day, nor a more flamboyant collection of daisies. The Japanese anemones are still lovely, and so are the Michaelmas daisies.*

The dahlias are still glorious — a mass of cold but promising buds.'

It is ridiculous, of course, for I am trying to write a truthful chronicle, not an Algernon Blackwood extravaganza. Yet, these are actual extracts from my diary, and the difference in their tone is due to Miss Hazlitt, and only to her.

She *knew*. She knew flowers not only by their names — English and Latin — not only by their families, nor their structures, nor their habits — she knew them in their essence. It is extraordinarily difficult to explain what I mean, but if you had seen her bend over a winter iris, you would realize what I meant. She pressed the ground about its roots, she fetched some gravel and scattered it on the earth, she helped it to shelter by slightly altering the position of the rock behind it. All these things could have been done by any gardener who is aware that the *Iris stylosa* needs 'a coarse, well-drained soil in a sheltered position.' But she knew more than that. There was a magic in her touch. At any rate, the iris over which she had bent was the only iris which bloomed that winter.

On the day after she arrived she was a new woman. I rejoiced. Yet, my gratification was tempered by a certain apprehension. I knew that as soon as she was strong enough, I should have to endure a religious cross-examination. I would not have minded this, on my own account, but I dreaded it, for fear of hurting her.

GARDEN FRIENDS

§IV

She had been with me for three days and I was still unsaved. The heart-to-heart talk had not yet taken place. Every time that we walked through the garden I felt that it was about to come.

'How can anyone look at that rose and fail to believe in God?'

This, I felt, was a flank attack. I looked at the rose and saw a huge earwig sitting in the middle of it.

'Or the devil!' I pointed to the earwig.

'Yes, yes indeed,' she said eagerly. 'We *must* believe in the devil.' (I wish I could recapture the yearning, the tremulous sincerity of her voice.) 'We are meant to believe in him. To believe in the devil is half way towards believing in — *Him!*' She had an extraordinary gift for making the capital H articulate.

I grunted, and tried to change the conversation. There was a lusty spray of groundsel at my feet. I bent down and tugged it up.

'These foul weeds . . .' I muttered.

'Oh but weeds are *wonderful!*' cried Miss Hazlitt. The tone of her voice robbed the remark of any sense of silliness or affectation. She meant what she said, with every fibre of her being. She went on: 'My father made a collection of Devonshire weeds which he presented to the Exeter museum. My sister Anna and I helped him to collect them. There was so much to learn, and they were often difficult to find, but some of them were so beautiful that we enjoyed it and felt it such a privilege to work with him.'

85

She refused to see ugly things . . . or perhaps it would be truer to say that she really did *not* see them . . . that her long training in looking on the bright side of things had made the dark actually invisible to her. One or two hideous little red brick bungalows had been put up in our village. I lamented their presence one day, when she came in from a walk.

'I did not see them' she said.

With anybody else I should have been extremely irritated by that remark. But I was not irritated with Miss Hazlitt, for I knew that she was telling the truth.

§ v

Toothache!

It was this grotesque and undignified affliction which gave her the cue for the little sermon which must inevitably be preached.

I will not endeavour to transcribe that sermon. Even if I could remember it, I should make it sound foolish. Perhaps it *was* foolish, divorced from her sweet accents. Yet there was a passage which can be transcribed without loss or humiliation, for in its stark simplicity it seemed to challenge the whole world in which I move and have my being . . . and perhaps the challenge may apply, equally, to you.

We had been talking . . . and talking. Words . . . they echoed and died away . . . they seemed to mean nothing. The lamp flickered. On the one side there was poverty and pain and faith, on the other there was plenty and health and . . .

I said to her, in desperation: 'But when you "came to," after the operation . . . when you woke up, in that awful agony, and they bent over you, and they said "we're very sorry, but you'll have to go through all this again" . . .'

'Yes?'

'When they told you the whole horrible business would have to be repeated . . .'

'Oh, I was so *thankful!*'

She broke in, unexpectedly. She was leaning forward and her hands were tightly clasped.

'You were . . . what?' I said it dully. I did not understand.

'Oh, but you *must* see. I was so thankful!'

'That it was all to happen again? That loathsome business?'

'Yes . . . yes! Because it meant that Christ was testing me . . . because . . .'

§ VI

My pen falters. There are some things which cannot be transcribed. The power, at any rate, is not mine. Perhaps it is just as well. For the sign of the cross is a sign that will not be denied . . . flash it across any page, saintly or secular, and the author is led on a wild chase of the will o' the wisp, is urged to explore the secret places of his soul, to cry out into the darkness around him, demanding witnesses for the prosecution or the defence.

And this, as I am constantly trying to remind myself, is a Garden Book.

But before I close this episode, I should like to record a little incident to which it led, some days later. It puts us all wrong, chronologically, but you will have to forgive that, for the incident concerns the Prime Minister, Mr. Ramsay MacDonald.

I was lunching with a delightful lady whose face, if it has not launched a thousand ships, has opened at least a thousand exhibitions, with the most appealing grace. The guest of honour was the Prime Minister.

They had served the brandy in huge glasses. It was cold outside. And anyway, I never had any self-control. So I told Mr. MacDonald what Miss Hazlitt had said, about being thankful that she had to have her teeth out a second time.

I remember the scene perfectly. It was all red and white. Red glasses on the table, bright red roses, a lovely red hat on my hostess's head, and quantities of women's red lips, eating raspberries out of season.

White walls, a white tablecloth, white cream splashing out of jugs which the footmen were handing round and the white hands and face of the Prime Minister, who was very tired.

I had told him the story, as I told it to you. And he said:

'Faith without works!'

He said it in such a strange, booming tone, and he heaved such a deep sigh after he had said it, that everybody stopped talking.

'*Faith Without Works!*' he repeated. Then he turned round and stared at me with eyes that seemed unutterably sad. What had the phrase recalled to him? How was he applying it? Was he thinking of his good companions, the wild men, who were at that very moment proclaiming, with embarrassing clarity, a similar doctrine? A doctrine of economic salvation, without any corresponding necessity to work for it? A creed of 'spend' without any accompanying warning to 'save'?

I don't know. All I know is that he stared at me, and said:

'Dead! That is what it is . . . her doctrine of Faith without Works . . . it is *dead!*'

And he took a glass of water, and drank it, neat.

§VII

Well, the religious battle ended somehow. Who won? Who knows? It does not matter. All I know is that Miss Hazlitt, during the rest of her visit, was just an enchanting person, who had learned much more about flowers than I shall ever learn.

Our walks were wonderful. During these walks she would talk, quietly but vividly, of the things around her, and often lovely sentences came from her lips. At least, they seemed lovely to me, echoing, as they did, quietly, in the autumn lanes. Thus, we passed a hedgerow that was fiery with hips and haws. She stopped and looked at them with bright, glistening eyes:

'A hard winter!' she said, putting her hand on my arm. 'Whenever I see the red berries growing so thickly, I know that a hard winter is coming. And I feel so thankful for God's provision for the birds . . .'

There is every conceivable argument against that statement . . . botanical, barometrical, ornithological. Yet one accepts it. Or rather, one would give one's soul to be able to accept it, for the spirit that inspired it gives to Nature a new and lovelier pattern. When she said it, the word 'red' suggested the obvious parallel — 'Nature red in tooth and claw.' Thus does the same colour send different radiations in different spirits.

§VIII

One walk, in particular, I remember. It was our last day together. And it was as though she were on her mettle . . . so many secrets did she reveal . . . so many tiny, vivid blossoms did she discover, trembling in the obscurity of a common hedge.

Nothing came to her amiss. It began to rain, and we were driven to shelter. I cursed the rain. 'But no,' she said 'I must not curse the rain. See how lovely were its pale shafts as they swept through the wind-tossed willows! And the leaves glistened . . . ah! like diamonds . . . in the sun. Besides the rain would be over soon . . .' She had hardly said it before there was a lull, and we set out again, over fields washed to a brighter green.

She reminded me of many things which I had forgotten. Here was a 'Robin's Cradle' . . . one of those crimson feathery balls which some weird insect makes in the secret branches of the sweet-briar. And here was a cluster of elderberries, and she told me an old recipe for elderberry wine.

Then suddenly she discovered, in a sheltered corner, a single belated scarlet pimpernel.

'Look!'

I looked. All I could think of to say was that the pimpernel was very late.

'Oh but don't you know about it?'

'What?'

She laughed. 'Of course, it mayn't be true . . . but I like to believe it is. Haven't you read *Gerard's Herball*?'

'Yes, but . . .' I wanted to know what all the mystery was about.

'I know it by heart!' Her eagerness was a delight to see. 'Listen . . .'

And here, to my great amazement and admiration, she recited, without a single mistake, a long passage from that exquisite volume, which was first published nearly three hundred years ago. In case any of my readers are unacquainted with it, I reproduce it here, as Miss Hazlitt recited it, and as it was originally written:

'Pimpernell is like unto Chickweed; the stalkes are foure square, trailing here and there upon the ground, whereupon do grow broad leaves: from the bosomes whereof come forth slender tendrels whereupon do grow small purple floures tending to rednesse.

'The female Pimpernell differeth not from the male in any one point, but in the colour of the floures; for like as the former hath reddish floures, this plant bringeth forth floures of a most perfect blew colour; wherein is the difference.

'They floure in Summer, and especially in the moneth of August, at what time the husbandmen having occasion to go unto their harvest worke, will first behold the floures of Pimpernell, whereby they know the weather that shall follow the next day after; as for example, if the floures be shut close up, it betokeneth raine and foule weather; contrariwise, if they be spread abroad, faire weather.'

At this point Miss Hazlitt paused: 'You see?' she said, 'They are spread abroad. That means fine weather.'

'Go on, please . . . please go on. Its the loveliest stuff I ever heard.'

She continued:

'Both the sorts of Pimpernell are of a drying faculty without biting, and somewhat hot, with a certaine drawing quality, insomuch that it doth draw forth splinters and things fixed in the flesh.'

And here she paused again.

'Is that all?'

'No.'

'Well?' I could not think why her eyes were twinkling so brightly, why such a strange smile lit her face.

'No, it is *not* all,' she repeated. 'The most wonderful part of all comes at the end. About the toothache. Listen.'

She took hold of my arm, and she finished the quotation:

'*The juyce cures the toothach being snift up into the nose-thrills, especially into the contrary nosethrill.*'

'Oh but it's uncanny,' I cried. 'The juyce cures the toothach. Its too good to be true.'

She bent down and touched the pimpernel gently, as though she would find some healing in the little red flowers.

'You must sniff it up into your nosethrill at once,' I demanded.

She turned and regarded me gravely. 'Especially into the contrary nosethrill,' she added.

At which, as Pepys would say, we were mightily amused.

We took the little pimpernel home. I do not know if she snift it up into the nosethrill, but when she left me, on the following day, the 'toothach' was cured.

Bless her!

And yet, from a strictly practical point of view, I am a little annoyed with Miss Hazlitt at the moment. For she has taken up a whole chapter, and I want to get on. But there are two other garden friends who have to be talked about first, as one of them, at least, is destined to play a considerable part in this book. We will meet her on the next page.

CHAPTER VII

GARDEN ENEMIES

§ 1

The garden still waits.

The wood . . . the greenhouse . . . the rock garden . . . still unchronicled! But it is not my fault. One thing leads to another. First it is a spray of winter jasmine that sends me off to chase its golden stars . . . then Miss Hazlitt intervenes, with her quiet smile. Soon, I do indeed believe, we shall be able to get down to business, and drop the wisest hints, and confess the most awful failures . . . (though we shall confess them with a slightly supercilious accent, since they belong to such a distant era). But first we must finish our introduction to the persons who influenced the development of the garden.

Which is the cue for the second entrance of Mrs. M.

Mrs. M. lives not fifty miles from me, but whether to the North, South, East or West, I prefer not to say. She is the only gardener I know who never, for one instant, recalls Ruth Draper. (I apologize for introducing that lady's name, but it had to come out, sooner or later.) Never does she walk down a border and say 'you should have seen this six weeks ago . . . the wallflowers were a *mass* . . . weren't they a mass,

94

Ada? . . . a positive *mass.*' Nor does she pause in front of a collection of feeble shoots and say 'of course, if you'd only come next month, I don't know what you would have *said* about these dahlias . . . what could he have said about the dahlias, Ada? . . . nobody *knows* what to say about them!'

Mrs. M. is not like that. I have tried to catch her garden off its guard, without success. I always seem to arrive at the crowning hour of something or other. I have a feeling that as my car draws up at the door the stocks blaze into their ultimate, purple flames, the last of the lilies open their scented lips, the final rose-bud sheds its virginity and flaunts itself in a southern breeze. Things are always at their very best when I visit Mrs. M. Perhaps if I stayed a little longer, till dusk fell, I might detect a weariness among the lilies, the stocks might droop, and on her hard pavements I might catch the echo of rose-leaves falling. But I can never stay long at Mrs. M's. She annoys me too much.

She is damnably efficient. She spends next to nothing on her garden, and gets astonishing results. She shows you a blaze of delphiniums. 'All out of a penny packet,' she croons. You pass a bank flaming with golden broom. 'All from seed,' she declares. 'A shilling packet I bought years ago.' In the rockery is a sheet of purple cyclamen. It grows so profusely on the hills outside Rome that the little boys stuff bundles of them on the backs of their bicycles, in the same way that English little boys load their backs with bluebells. 'Just a few roots I stuffed into my

95

suitcase after my visit to Italy last year,' she murmurs.

And one is sure that she went to Italy for about ten shillings, and picked up a Guardi or a Bronzino for a couple of lire, and had a suite of rooms for which she paid half a crown a night.

She bullies one. The first time she came to see me she cried 'Oh — but you must have a lavender hedge. Why haven't you got a lavender hedge? And I can't see any scarlet lupins. You *must* have scarlet lupins . . . so easy to grow . . . I have masses . . . I'll send you some seeds.'

If she does, they will go down the drain, damn her.

'And your rock roses . . . where did you get them?'

Scenting a compliment, I told her.

'How much did you pay for them?'

Again I told her.

'But that's *monstrous*!' She poked her umbrella contemptuously into the middle of my best clump: 'It's daylight robbery. You shouldn't pay a quarter of that. And in any case, why do you want to pay for them at all, when you can get quantities wild near Sandringham?'

'But Sandringham's fifty miles away.'

'You've got a car, haven't you? All you need to do is to take a trowel and a fork, get into your car, and come back with enough to stock your garden.'

'One day the Queen will catch you at it, and put you in the Tower,' I observed, bitterly.

Whereupon, to my disgust, she broke into a high, hard laugh, and said 'How funny you are? You must write that down!'

Well — I have written it down, but not quite in the way she expected.

Mrs. M's most irritating trait is that she is always right. When I was beginning my little winter garden, she went round it, shaking her head, and saying in tones of the utmost relish 'Oh I'm afraid this will never *do* here . . . it might be all right in Cornwall . . . but here it will never *do*.'

'Never do what?' I asked. She makes one deliver feeble jokes like that.

Of course, the things which she had indicated didn't 'do'. But I feel that at least part of their failure was due to the fact that Mrs. M. had cast an evil spell over them. Her spirit was like a chill breath, withering everything which it touched.

Mrs. M. in short, was a witch. We had better leave it at that.

§ 11

I will call my next garden acquaintance Undine Wilkins, because it is the sort of bastard name she ought to have had . . . a sickly æstheticism grafted on to a plebeian stock.

Because she is very thick-skinned, she will not recognize herself, and I should not greatly care if she did, for she is rich, thoroughly self-satisfied, and now lives in the Colonies.

She arrived with a charming friend of mine, on to whom she had attached herself like a pale but deter-

G

mined leech. She stayed for a week. Both my friend
and I were driven to the verge of hysteria by her
posing and her terrible determination to 'appreciate'
things, but what could one do? One could not turn
her out. I dropped hints, on more than one occasion,
that other guests were expected, but she only opened
her eyes innocently and said 'who?' And, as I could
never think of anybody, on the spur of the moment,
but the Aga Khan (for whom she appeared to entertain a peculiar passion); this ruse cannot be described
as very successful.

'Oh . . . oh . . . but it's Honeymoon Cottage!
. . .' she cried, clasping her hands, and opening her
mouth very wide, as she first stepped into my garden.

There is no reply to this sort of remark, so I did a
sort of gurgle.

'No . . . no . . .' she breathed, putting one hand
over her eyes 'don't . . . don't say anything. Listen.'

I listened. All I could hear were some pigs making
slightly obscene noises in a neighbouring farm. I
looked at her enquiringly. Had she a pig complex,
or something?

'The peace of it,' she hissed, 'the peace!'

She drew a long drawn sigh, and opened her eyes
again. Her eyelids fluttered madly for a moment.
Then, like a brave little thing, she forced a smile to
her lips, drew my arm through hers, and murmured,
'show me . . . show me . . . *everything.*'

Checking the indelicate thought that she was
making 'a certain suggestion' to me (as the Sunday
newspapers would say), I showed her round the

garden. It was agony. For she had the curious illusion, entertained by so many affected women, that her ignorance was charming. She would poke her parasol into a clump of lupins, to their infinite peril, and say 'lovely . . . *lovely* canterbury bells!' I began by correcting her, but I soon desisted, because I found that she said these things merely in order to be corrected, so that she might mince about and giggle and say 'what a little town mouse I am!' (she said this quite often, and she pronounced it 'toon moose').

So finally, when she pushed her rather large and thickly powdered nose into a bush of honeysuckle, murmured 'divine jasmine', and looked at me over her shoulder for the expected correction, I did not play up. I said 'Yes, isn't it?' She looked quite hurt . . . like a child deprived of its toy.

After she had been with us for two days, her affectations became almost intolerable. She was always posing in ultra-old-world positions all over the garden. While one was squashing beetles or pulling up weeds she would drape herself against a tree or a bush, fondly imagining that she thereby enhanced its beauty. We had many acid little dialogues in such circumstances.

I remember one morning when she had extended herself in an extremely artful pose in front of a lovely wistaria. I was grovelling after wire-worms. I looked up and saw her.

She (looking at the wistaria but really referring to herself): What a picture!

Me: Yes.

She: Like tassels of silk, aren't they?

Me: Are they? I can't see. You're standing in front of them.

She (laughing gaily): I *must* have my background.

Me (seizing a huge wire-worm and squashing it with relish): As long as you don't lean against it, you're welcome.

At which she would pout, toss her head and wander off.

I never knew a woman who took so many impedimenta into a garden. She had, for example, a huge hat with ribbons, which she swung girlishly over one arm.

'This is for making hay,' she giggled.

'It looks as if it were made of hay already.'

'Oh let's . . . let's make hay . . . now! Lots of it.'

I would very much have liked, at that moment, to take her by the neck and rub her nose in an ants' nest. Instead, like a perfect gentleman, I said 'Hay isn't made till July.' Then I added hastily, 'At least, I think it is. At any rate it isn't made in June.'

'Oh but let's make it *earlier* . . . and sell it . . . and make lots and lots of money!'

She also had a huge shallow basket, of beige-coloured straw with a pale blue ribbon threaded round the sides. It was a silly, vilely unpractical basket. Everything fell out of it. One would have had to be a conjuror to balance more than half a dozen roses in it. And she was no conjuror. Moreover, she was always in a semi-drugged mental state, because she considered it right to be 'affected' by beauty. She therefore loitered about the garden — (if she thought anybody was looking) swinging the basket slowly, and the poor roses were scattered in her wake, their petals bruised and their stems broken.

In her, the vulgar townswoman's condescension to the country was developed to the highest degree. This surprised me because, in worldly matters, she was not utterly a fool. Yet, here she was, a snob, a climber, a would-be member of the 'smart' society, uttering gurgles of silly surprise and affected excitement at the most ordinary country customs . . . as, for example, the pleasant manner in which the villagers wished me 'good morning'.

'*Quite* the squire, aren't you,' she exclaimed gaily. 'I *never* realized . . . I thought they were all *Bolsheviks* . . . what a little toon moose I am!'

I must repeat that this attitude . . . in an otherwise accomplished climber . . . surprised me. I could not think why she should imagine that her arch urbanity — I use the word in its literal sense — was 'smart'. Surely she must have realized that most of the women whose society she claimed so eagerly were just as much at home in the country as the town? Surely she must have known that most of them had country houses, and loved their gardens and their dogs and their tweeds? So, at least, I reasoned. But I never solved the problem.

She had travelled a little . . . a winter on the Riviera, one or two flustered expeditions to Paris, where she had stayed at the Hotel du Gard de Nord (in mind as well as in body). There had also been a flouncing sort of walking tour down the Rhine with a girl friend. These expeditions had given to her vocabulary an awful cosmopolitanism. She would pause before some object, flick her fingers, and say with wistful regret, 'oh dear, how *does* one say it in English?'

For example, she walked with me down a brilliant yellow-edged border one day, and pointed vaguely to the flowers at her feet.

'Divine!' she murmured. 'These *giroflets*. How does one say them in English?'

Perversely I pretended not to understand. 'How does one say which?'

'These . . .' she repeated, 'these divine *giroflets!*'

'One says wallflowers,' I replied bluntly. 'Unless one is tight. Then one says nothing at all.'

She laughed her worst sort of laugh — the high 'bird-like' one — and the incident passed over.

But before many minutes had elapsed she was at it again. This time, Germany claimed her. She began to talk, much against my will, about my own work. I do not mind writing about my own work but I heartily detest talking about it. However, she would not be deterred.

'Of course, I liked *Prelude* best of all your novels,' she said.

Now this, in itself, was the most depressing thing she could possibly have said. To tell any author that you like his first book better than any of his others is equivalent to telling him that his entire literary career has been one long degeneration. It casts a blight over a man. It cast a definite blight over me. I

shoved my hands deeper in my pockets and muttered
'Oh!'

'Yes,' she said, 'it seemed to me so . . . so . . .'

'So what?' I wondered which language she would
choose next.

'So *sympathetisch geschrieben* . . . that's what I mean
. . . how *does* one say it in English?'

I glared at her with a steely eye . . . at least, I hope
it was steely. I said 'I know very little German, but I
do know that *geschrieben* means "written" and I
would hazard a wild guess that *sympathetisch* meant
"sympathetically." Putting two and two together,
I think we might safely conclude that it meant
"sympathetically written." Is that what you intended
to say?'

'Yes,' she sighed. 'And no. One can't analyse
these things can one?'

I was baffled by this remark, and said nothing.
Nor had I any need. For she capped her remarks
about *Prelude* by comparing it to another public
school novel, and, in my opinion, a very boring
one.

'It has the same delicate bloom on it. . . .' she said,
'the same lovely adolescence. Have you read it?'

'Yes.'

'Oh tell me . . . tell me what you think of it?'

'I think,' I replied, 'that it is *tripe à la mode*. But
I cannot imagine how one would say that in English.'

CHAPTER VIII

HOW NOT TO MAKE A ROCK GARDEN

§ 1

WE have dallied long enough with Miss Hazlitt, Miss Wilkins and Mrs. M. But the dalliance really was necessary, for it was entirely through the goading of Mrs. M. that I made my first great experiment . . . the rock garden.

By 'first great experiment' I mean my first real structural work. I had weeded and dug and planted but I had not built nor scooped nor trifled with the landscape. I was now destined to trifle quite a lot.

When I first came to the cottage, I decided that there would not be a rock garden at all. Partly because there seemed no place where such a garden could be made, but principally because, in my ignorance, I did not greatly care for rock gardens.

I have not a 'rock garden mind'. Until quite recently I associated rock gardens with the horrors of the English Riviera . . . visualized them as gaunt, damp rubbish heaps on Southern promenades, over which there brooded a few diseased palms, while, in front of them, passed an endless procession of nurse-maids, wheeling perambulators in which revolting infants glowered and spat.

Rock gardens seemed to be the monopoly of

garden gossip-writers, who were always telling one to tidy up the saxifrages, and throw snails over the left shoulder. I had, in short, the gloomiest views about rock gardens, and, as previously stated, it was only by accident that I ever possessed one.

It happened like this. The first summer which I ever enjoyed in my cottage was phenomenally dry. Day after day one looked up to skies of enamelled blue, praying for rain. But no rain came. Sinister cracks appeared in the herbaceous borders. The roses drooped flushed exhausted heads. Even the pansies protruded purple tongues over the crumbling earth, demanding mercy.

For several anxious weeks I scrambled about the neighbourhood in search of water. There was a pond in a distant field which was often raided, at dusk, when its owner was safely in the local pub. I would set off, accompanied by any friends who were staying with me, and make many guilty excursions to this pond. How exciting was the gurgle of the water as one thrust the pails into the cool mud! How exquisite the smooth glitter of the water as one poured it into the welcoming tank in the greenhouse! Till late at night we would labour, the sweat pouring off our foreheads, scurrying silently over the fields, cursing softly as the pail made an indiscreet clatter, thinking always of the dry, dying roots which we were so soon to succour.

Very pretty and adventurous, you will agree. But also extremely inconvenient. After a few nights of scurrying and being thoroughly boyish, we were bored, and decided that it was really far more agreeable to sit at home and play bridge, and drink brandy like civilized persons. It was, therefore, decided, as we laid away the last pail, somewhat sulkily at midnight, that the water problem must be solved by the creation of a pond.

§ 11

It was the creation of this pond which led, by steps which will shortly be explained, to the creation of the rock garden. First, however, please note that the episode of the pond was the one occasion on which I ever triumphed over my father. *I* said that if one dug a very deep hole in the earth, a pond would eventually come and sit in the hole. *He* said that no pond would come, that the earth would fall in, and the water would run away. Well, the earth did not fall in and the water did not run away. Indeed the water rose at such a rate that we had to dig trenches to prevent the whole garden from being flooded. But that is another matter. The fact remains that I was right about the pond and my father was wrong. He never passes by it without slightly curling his nostrils, and making a noise strangely like that charming Victorian interjection . . . 'pshaw!'

The pond was dug by a young man from a neighbouring village. There was a legend that he was very lazy, and that he must be watched if any work was to be got out of him. And so I would be constantly popping out of the house and peering at him over the hedge, in the fond expectation that my awful presence would galvanize him into greater activity. Unfortunately, it had precisely the opposite effect, for he conceived an almost morbid fancy for me. As soon as he saw me, sternly regarding him, he would drop his spade, fold his arms, and gaze up in a sort of ecstasy. The fiercer my expression the more captivating he appeared to find it. 'Always got a smoile for a poor chap, aven't 'ee, sir?' he would croon . . . or words to that effect. I learnt, from other sources, that this affection was genuine, and that he continued to sing my praises when he got home, to the great annoyance of his wife. So I decided that it would be better not to pop out any more, but to trust to his affection from a distance.

Before the pond had reached any appreciable depth, I had to return to London, and it was more than a month before I was able to be at Allways again. Judge, therefore, of my surprise when I discovered, as I hurried over the field, that I had created not only a pond but a mountain. This mountain towered over the pond in a most menacing manner. It had not previously occurred to me that if you dig a large hole, the earth from the hole will ascend at the same rate that the hole descends. It occurred to me very forcibly now, and I did not like it at all.

Now, at all moments of crisis in my country life Mrs. M. has a habit of popping up, and I had hardly seen the mountain, and was still wondering where I could possibly put it, when a footstep on the other side of the hedge betrayed her presence.

'Ah . . . good evening! Going for a climb up Mont Blanc? He! He! Ho! Ho!'

I turned and said, with grave distaste, 'Good evening, Mrs. M.' Then I averted my eyes from her, and drew from my pocket a piece of paper on which I pretended to make notes. I did not wish to make notes, and actually I only wrote the word 'William' over and over again. But I wrote it very firmly, frowning as I did so, in the hope that Mrs. M. would go away.

Mrs. M. did not go away. Far from it. She actually slipped through the hedge as though she had been invited. I wrote 'William' once again, very hastily, and folded up the paper.

She stared at it inquisitively. 'Making Notes?'

I shook my head, and smiled.

Baffled, she snorted. Then, very heartily she said 'You'll have a job getting all this earth away, what?'

'Getting it away?'

'Well . . . you're surely not going to leave it here . . . like this?'

'Not like this . . . no.' My mind was working with desperate speed to try to get some valid reason for keeping the earth. Now that I had given Mrs. M. the impression that I was not going to move the earth, I was determined to keep it there.

Then suddenly I had an inspiration. 'This,' I blurted out, 'is the beginning of my rock garden.'

And it was.

§III

Mrs. M. stared at me with undisguised suspicion. 'Rock garden?' she cried. 'What do you mean . . . rock garden?'

'By a rock garden,' I replied, 'I mean a garden containing a quantity of rocks.'

'But you haven't any rocks.'

'Not yet . . . no.'

'Where are you going to get them?'

I had not the least idea where I was going to get them, so I said, in a sepulchral voice 'They Are Coming,' rather as though the skies might open at any moment and deluge us with a cascade of boulders.

'Yes . . . but where from?'

'Yorkshire.' This was partly guess-work and partly memory, because I remembered reading in some book of a man who had a quarry of stone in Yorkshire which he used to export.

Mrs. M. snorted again. 'That'll cost you a pretty penny,' she said. I could hear signs of fierce envy in her voice. She swung her string-bag backwards and forwards, and glared at my mountain. Then she said:

'But you're surely not just going to stuff a lot of rocks on all that mud?'

'Stuff them? No. I shan't stuff them.'

'Well . . . throw them, then. You've got to have some sort of design.'

'I have.'

'What is it?'

'It is being Done For Me,' I said.

'By whom?'

I could think of nobody but Sir Edwin Lutyens, who designed Delhi. So I said 'You will catch cold, Mrs. M., if you stand in the wet grass.'

I am glad to be able to record that she did.

§ I V

I was therefore committed to a rock garden. I spent a restless night, cursing myself for being so easily irritated by Mrs. M. But on the following morning, when I again visited the pond and its accompanying mountain, the prospect did not look so black. The site was promising. A fair slope led down to the pond. Two green arms of a hedge encircled it. And over the pond towered the mountain, which had only to be slightly sat on, and carven into shape, and decorated with roses, cunningly disposed, to be transformed into a rock garden.

So I fondly imagined.

I ordered the rocks. I was told that it was cheaper to order a truck-full, which would contain about eight tons. It seemed a great deal, especially as they had to come all the way from Yorkshire. However I was assured that if less were ordered 'it would come out much dearer in the end'. This commercial principle is usually to be distrusted, for we learn by bitter experience that it is not cheaper to order, for example, ten yards of silk for pyjamas when only three are required, or to buy a guinea bottle of hair oil when the three-shilling size would do just as well. For it usually happens that we take a hatred to the silk, while the oil goes bad. However, it was unlikely that the rocks would go bad. Besides, there constantly rose before me the sneering face of Mrs. M. who did not believe that any rocks were coming at all.

She believed it, well enough, a few days later, when she had to drive four miles out of her way because the road in front of my cottage was completely blocked by the collapse of an enormous van-full of best quality, fully weathered Yorkshire rocks. She believed it still more when she discovered that she would be deprived of the services of her odd man, who had secretly deserted her in order to earn double pay in transporting my rocks across the field. He had transported them with such energy that he ruptured himself, and was confined to his bed for three weeks.

At last the thing was done. All the rocks were safely ensconced in the mountain . . . the big ones at the bottom, the small ones at the top. Looking back at this adventure, it seems almost incredible that I could have been such a fatuous and ignorant optimist as to imagine that this was the way to make a rock garden . . . without any plan, without even an adequate preparation of the soil. Yet, I did imagine it . . . until I saw it in being. Then I realized that a very big and expensive mistake had been made.

The thing was horrible. It was utterly out of keeping with the quiet and rambling beauty of the rest of the garden. I tried looking at it from this way and from that, half closing my eyes and putting my head on one side. I regarded it before and after cocktail-time. It looked much worse after, which is a proof that alcohol stimulates the æsthetic sense. No amount of self-hypnotism could persuade me that I liked it.

It reminded me of those puddings made of sponge-cake and custard, which are studded with almonds until they look like some dreadful beast thrown up from the depths of the sea. It had no sort of design. It was so steep that the earth was already showing signs of falling away in the slightest rain. The best I could say about it was that it made a very good shelter from the wind.

Had it not been for Mrs. M. I should have destroyed it overnight. False pride made me keep it there for several days. But there are stronger emotions than false pride. One morning, a few days later, I went out, saw the hideous thing and decided that it could remain no longer. Urgently we summoned the same men who had put it together. By the following afternoon, the earth had all been taken away, and deposited in a neighbouring field. There remained only a quantity of rocks, scattered about the grass.

CHAPTER IX

THE OTHER SIDE OF THE PICTURE

§ I

AND now I found myself confronted by the first real problem of my gardening career.

Here were the rocks, the grass, the pond. Here was I, standing in a flat field, wondering what on earth could be done with them. How could they possibly be made to fit in with the landscape . . . how could one ever hope that they would ever look anything but a lot of rocks in a field? For days these questions presented themselves. And no answer was forthcoming.

Now, when you ask yourself a question and do not receive an answer, you must do something about it. You must not sit still, in a paralysing silence. So I decided to do something as quickly as possible. The thing I did was to order three Scotch pines.

I ordered three Scotch pines for several reasons. Partly because it was November, and partly because I like Scotch pines, but principally because Scotch pines 'went' with rocks, and I hoped that they might help me to find some sort of design.

They did. One was planted on the very edge of the pond. That suggested a little hill behind it. The other two were planted a little distance away. Which suggested a tiny valley, leading to a second hill. Thus, a vague idea of a topographical outline had been born. That was the first hurdle which had to be surmounted.

However there were many others. The Scotch pines were duly placed in their appointed positions. We began to delve and to build. Then we remembered that the pines would eventually grow, and cast shade, and we had to move them to a different position. More delving and more building. Then we discovered that the roots of the Scotch pines were too near the water and would probably rot. They had to be moved again. They were moved, in all, five times. An expression of poignant fatigue hovered over their branches when they reached their final resting place.

Then we found that we had not enough rocks. We ordered more. Then it transpired that the top-soil of loam and sand was not nearly deep enough, that it was only a feeble coating over the hard clay; all the rocks had to be taken up again, more earth had to be removed, more cartloads of sandy loam delivered. Oh, it is great stuff, this rock-gardening! It would be unutterably tedious to narrate the innumerable stages through which we progressed. I can best sum it up by suggesting a few elemental rules for the guidance of those who are even more ignorant than myself.

When you are making a Rock Garden:

1. You must be bloody, bold and resolute. By this I mean that you must stand at a little distance from your slope, visualize a certain broad design, and decide there and then to carry out that design, cost what it may. Perhaps you want a little valley, that

rises gently to a little hill. If so, you must mark the outline of that valley, there and then, with sticks or stones, or whatever may come handy, and get your gardener to come along to help you scoop it out. Long before you have attained the desired outline you will feel sick of the whole thing. You will feel that you have descended into the bowels of the earth before you have done much more than scratch the surface. But you must stick to it. Otherwise your rock garden will have no design at all.

2. You must be monstrously extravagant with your rocks. By which I mean that you must push them really deep into the earth. It is agony to have to do this, because a big rock probably costs about five shillings, when you come to reckon up the price of its transport, the labour of the men who put it in, etc. It would be much more soothing to stick the rock on the top of the slope so that you could say 'Look at my enormous rock! How rich I am to be able to afford such enormous rocks!' But if you do stick the rock up like that, you will eventually take a hatred to it. Also, nothing will grow on it, and anyway it will certainly fall down. So really, you must bury it so that only a mossy nose sticks out. It is maddening to have to do a thing like that.

However, as the garden writers would say, '*it is advisable to follow the dictates of Nature, which, being natural, is the amateur's wisest guide. Nature, whom the Greeks worshipped, is just as possible to reproduce in the humblest suburban garden as in the lofty palaces of the duke. The rocks should be buried to two-thirds of their cubic capacity in rich, well-seasoned loam, to which a small proportion of sand has been administered.'* Garden authors really do write like that. I envy them their style. There is the echo of a healthy, well-spent life in every paragraph.

3. Having obtained your design, and buried your rocks, your next task is to exercise phenomenal restraint about the things which you put in. I have always been a fervent advocate of birth-control, but since I have been the owner of a rock garden my fervour has increased a hundred-fold. The prolificacy of the common saxifrage is positively embarrassing. The speed with which the rock rose reproduces itself brings a blush to the cheek. Violas appear to have absolutely no self-control, and as for the alyssum . . . well, if *we* behaved like the alyssum, Australia would be over-populated before the year is out.

Forgive me . . . I ought not to have spoken disparagingly of the generosity of these delightful plants. It is really rather caddish to sneer at a saxifrage which climbs, so bravely, from rock to rock, bearing its sweet standards aloft, carrying to the barren lands a rosy glow of hope. How can a decent man check the glowing flame of violas, that burn ever more blue in successive dawns, spreading their cold fire in secret places? These are valiant flowers, and gay, and sturdy, and it is only one's own decadence which urges one to decry them. For us, the rocks are not so easily scaled, nor the darkness so sweetly illuminated.

§ 11

A plague on sentimentality. There has been quite enough 'pretty writing' for the moment.

We have set down the three main rules to be observed while one is making a rock garden. We can now return to the narrative.

During the whole time that the rock garden, in its revised version, was made, I was driven to distraction by the visits of neighbouring acquaintances, who seemed to entertain a strange illusion that my rock garden was public property. One of the most irritating of these visitors was Undine Wilkins. You may remember her in a previous chapter, mincing about the garden, pretending to be very thrilled by beauty – posing, always posing. (In case you forget her, she was in the habit of calling herself a 'town mouse,' which she pronounced 'toon moose.')

Miss Wilkins had taken a cottage in our village for the winter, and she was sharing it with a very peculiar-looking woman who had a black moustache and wore a high, stiff collar. I shall call her Miss Q. I understand that Miss Q. had a very winning way with girl guides. However I very seldom saw her.

La Belle Undine minced across my field one morning soon after the disappearance of the mountain. She was the very last person whom I wished to see, because there were a great many things to think about . . . the gradients of the slopes, drainage problems, the precise depth at which the rocks should be placed, etc. Strict concentration was necessary, and Undine was hardly of the type which helps a man to concentrate.

'Oh let *me* put a rock in . . .' she cried, skipping forward like an intoxicated lamb. 'Just *one!* May I? *Please?*'

She was breathing very hard in my face, and her mouth was like a damp raspberry jujube, and she was just oozing with 'allure.' In desperation I said 'Yes, yes . . . please put a rock in!'

She tossed her head, and gave me a terrific look.

Then she approached a very small rock, and extended her lily-white fingers over it.

'Ooh!' she cried.

'What is it? Have you squashed a slug?'

'Oh, but it's a *mountain!*'

I said nothing. It was a rock about the size of a small cabbage. La Belle Undine, had she desired, could have seized it between her teeth . . . which were large . . . and tossed it into position. But she did not so desire. She had a Plan.

The plan was that I should come forward, diffidently, and apply my bulging muscles to the removal of the rock. While I was doing this our hands would touch, whereupon she would flush, and bite her lip, and toss her head. Then, like a perfect gentleman, I would offer her my handkerchief to wipe the mud off.

But I am not a perfect gentleman, my muscles do not bulge inordinately, and my handkerchiefs are very expensive. So that I did not come forward, as desired. Undine had to move the rock into position

SUMMER

all by herself. She did this with many pouts and carefully simulated gasps, rather in the manner of those strong women of the music halls, who stagger about with hollow cannon balls, registering Effort.

When she had finished she straightened herself, tossed a truant lock from her forehead, and surveyed the rock garden with very large eyes.

'Oh, but it's a quarry!' she cried.

She clasped her hands together, and gazed ecstatically at the behind of a young man who was lifting a rock into position. The young man dropped the rock and glared round at her as though she was about to sting him.

Not at all deterred, she minced a little nearer.

'A quarry!' she repeated, and then gazed at me, with parted lips.

Now, what does one do when that sort of woman makes that sort of remark? Does one skip about with lowered eyelids, and murmur, politely, 'a quarry, a quarry, I've got a blasted quarry'? Or does one throw back the head, and laugh nonchalantly, and say 'Oh *no*, Miss W . . . just a few pebbles'? Or does one say nothing at all, but give a look, which will make Miss W. think that you desire to do outrageous things to her in a quarry? Who can say? It is beyond me, especially when the grass is long and wet, and one is trying to persuade oneself that one's rock garden does not look like a seaside grotto.

So I said nothing at all. I hoped that a campaign of dignified silence would eventually drive La Belle Undine away. It did not do so, because she chose

to interpret the silence as masculine embarrassment
. . . I was tongue-tied, she presumed, at the sight of
her, fluttering about among the rocks, patting the
earth here, pressing a delicate heel there. Actually
I was thinking how easy it would be to drop a rock
on her neck and end this persecution.

She fluttered about, like a tiresome, yapping dog,
throughout the entire progress of my rock garden.
Even when it was finished, I had not done with her,
for a few days later she sent me a horrible little tree
in a pink pot, 'for the rockery.' I love almost every
tree and shrub that grows, except the 'monkey puzzle,'
the speckled laurel, and another one whose name I
have never learnt. It was this abomination which she
had chosen to send me. It had shiny leaves of an
ugly shade of green, and it was covered with slimy-
looking orange berries. It was obviously created by
God to serve as a cheap Christmas present.

Accompanying it was a note on very scented paper,
with the address of her cottage peeping out from
among the flourishes of a gigantic crest. At the end of
every sentence she had placed at least one exclamation
mark, and usually three. Anybody who read it would
imagine, from its breathless and ecstatic style, that La
Belle Undine had rolled about with me in the rocks
until we were both bruised beyond recognition.

'I simply *had* to buy him!' she wrote. 'Those sweet
little orange balls. . . .'

But I really must reach for the blotting paper. . . .

§III

You will find, as you wander through your garden life, that each form of gardening has its separate and peculiar charm . . . that one corner of your garden will evoke a mood quite distinct from that which pervades you in another. A large garden is like a large house, with rooms variously decorated. There are rooms which soothe and rooms which stimulate, rooms that are only made for work and rooms that are only made for play. The clearest analogy that occurs to me is between the kitchen and the kitchen garden . . . in both these places there is the same feeling of comfort and security. The same tranquillity lurks in the smell of sultanas on a shelf as in the cool tang of a cabbage in a roughly dug patch.

The charm of a rock garden is essentially Lilliputian. To extract the keenest pleasure from it you must be able to diminish yourself — you must acquire the talent for shrivelling yourself up into a creature that is able to walk, in spirit, under the tiny saxifrages, and shiver with alarm at their heavy weight of blossom, to climb, in your mind's eye, the mossy stones, and grow dizzy on their steep escarpments. This is the whole genius of the rocks . . . the power they have to swell out and out, until they are full of menace.

Endless adventures of the spirit are possible in the rock garden, if you have an hour to spare, and are free from Mrs. M's and Miss W's. There is every stimulus to the imagination. The smallest pool in a rock's hollow becomes a great lake, and a clump of

123

violas is transformed into a pathless jungle. In the valley where the rock roses grow the sun never comes, but it is wild with splendour over the crest of the aubretias . . . far, far away. And thus, when you are designing your rock garden, though you must be sternly practical in many things, it is as well sometimes to allow your fancy the freest flight . . . to place certain plants simply for their 'adventurous' value, i.e. to put a miniature pine, six inches high, at the top of a small mound, so that you have all the fun of thinking that it is a forest giant on a mountain summit.

The first really big experiment I ever tried in my rock garden was the result of just such a childish excursion. It was concerned with a group of *Chionodoxa*. (If you look it up in the *Encyclopædia of Gardening* you will find that its other name is Glory of the Snow, that it is of the order of *Liliaceæ*, that it is a hardy, deciduous bulbous plant, and that it was 'first introduced' in 1877.)

The experiment, as I say, was due to a happy accident. One day I was weeding. There were a lot of peculiarly loathsome docks, against which I had declared war. Docks are the worst weeds of all, because just as you are pulling them up, they make a sickly, sucking noise, and break in half. The root remains in the ground, and you find yourself clinging on to the leaf. Whereupon you have to tramp off to the tool shed, arm yourself with a trowel, and return to the scene of action, only to find that you have forgotten where the abominable dock-root is lurking. In a rage, you scrape up a lot of earth, feeling like a dog that has lost a bone, and if you are lucky you will find, after ten minutes' search, an obscene sprout that you imagine to be the dock root. It is only after you have thrown it into the hedge that you realize, with horror, that you have destroyed your best gentian. The only person of my acquaintance who ever said a good word for docks was Miss Hazlitt. She told me that if you rubbed their leaves on your skin after you had been stung by a nettle, the poison would disappear. And also that a dock leaf was an ideal wrapping for butter.

Well, I was bending down over the docks for quite a long time, and when I occasionally looked up, I saw the world upside down. And then, all of a sudden, a little lump of earth detached itself from the top of the slope, and rolled slowly down to my feet. It was only a very little lump, the size of a plum, but in my Lilliputian mood it seemed immense. I stepped back quickly, as though to escape from an avalanche. As soon as I thought of the avalanche I thought also how wonderful it would be if I *could* simulate an avalanche here, with flowers of white and frosty blue, foaming down from the summit to form a great pool at the bottom.

It occurs to me that this is possibly a very long and elaborate explanation of a very minor event . . . minor even in the chronicle of my garden, for the avalanche when completed was only a few feet long. However, it seems that one becomes Lilliputian in one's style, merely by thinking of the rock garden.

I spent one of the happiest mornings of my life

planting the bulbs of the chionodoxa. They were such nice bulbs. Round and smooth and clean, like nuts. I would have eaten one of them, had I not been so conscientious. Moreover, on the day when I planted them I was in a particularly good 'shrinking' mood. I had only to narrow my eyes and to think hard for a moment, to become two inches high, to gaze in becoming awe at the rocks over which my hands were spread. There are some days when it is terribly difficult to shrink properly. Try as one will, one remains six foot high. . . . a cumbersome human in an overcoat, with cold feet and a trowel. But to-day . . . ah, my body was as volatile as the ghostly scarlet leaves of the maple near by, that stained the October sky with swift bloodstains. . . .

Never was there such fun. I made a little plan of it all. At the top of the slope I laid a mass of bulbs to represent the gathering snow. In order that the illusion might be perfect, I chose the smallest bulbs for this position, and packed them very tight. Then, where two rocks jutted out, I made my avalanche split in two. There would be a foam of blossom on either side, breaking here, flowing there, sweeping turbulently over the brown soil. And then, where the main rock jutted out, I seized bulbs by the handful, and jammed them in all round, in order that there might be a fierce jet and spray of blossom. This accomplished, I paused. But not for long. For there were many minor rivulets to be created, many pale streams to bring into being, wandering in irregular lines through the small boulders, till they ended in a little pool of earth into which I placed the last of the bulbs, hoping so earnestly that one day the pool would be blue, and restless with blossom.

For many weeks I visited that patch of sloping ground where the chionodoxa lay dormant. My diary is full of impatient entries about it. Thus:

November 30th. No sign of chionodoxa. Feel very depressed. Doubt if shall ever succeed in anything.

December 15th. No sign of chionodoxa. Why do I live in this damned country? Had a letter from Willie Maugham to-day. They are bathing at Antibes.

January 18th. No sign of chionodoxa. If the government goes on spending money at this rate, there will be a flight from the pound.

February 3rd. No sign of chionodoxa. My hair is coming out. Went yesterday to hair man, says must have treatment. Will cost twelve guineas.

March 3rd. No sign of chionodoxa. Perhaps I should feel better if I had a real religion. But how *can* one have a real religion if one *wants* to have one so much? I mean, does not the *desire* in itself nullify the authenticity of the creed . . . which means nothing . . . but I am so terribly tired, that I cannot phrase things properly.

March 10th. Signs of chionodoxa! Really, at last, three wart-like objects have appeared. They are so late that one ought to have hit them on the head and told them to go back, and come again next year. But one doesn't. Is one weak?

March 20th. *Two chionodoxa out!* Ah, but it was

worth waiting for! The most beautiful blue. Like the blue of a church window on a cold spring morning when the sun is behind it, and the starlings are shrill outside the porch. But I must not go on like this.

I must not indeed. If I am to keep any remnants of my soul intact, for future serial publication, I must shut up that diary with a snap. Yet, I cannot shut it up before I recall those early delights in my avalanche . . . delights which were endless in the lengthening twilights of spring, as I bent down, and looked up at the nodding spray of blossom, descending just as I had planned, a rivulet here, a cascade there, and a grand torrent in the middle over the central rock, all outlined against the deep, quiet skies of April. For my avalanche was an avalanche that really succeeded, that swept into my memory, for ever.

§ I V

It would be absurd presumption on my part if I were to attempt to offer any hints on the creation or the maintenance of rock gardens, since my own knowledge is so very limited. But in its very limitation lies a certain value. If you have only been doing a thing for a few years the memory of early blunders has not lost its sting, and the memory of early triumphs is still fresh about you.

My first triumph . . . or rather, my first little splash of colour, was an aubretia. It sounds comparatively tame but I do pray you not to neglect the aubretias, for of all the flowers I know, they are the kindest.

There are few months in the year when you cannot find some colour on them. I write in October, when my aubretias still hold many trembling, purple stars, and I remember that from March to May they gave me delight with their thick cushions of blossom.

But their floribundity — if there is such a word — is only a small part of their claim to our respect. They are, of all plants, the easiest to increase. Tear off a piece of root, press it in the earth, and it unfailingly thrives. This, at least, has been my experience. Moreover, the flowers are far more valuable for cutting than most of us imagine. People see the frail tiny petals, they explore downwards and discover a straggly stalk that is like a thread of cotton, and they shake their heads, thinking that the petals would be shed before dawn, and that the narrow stalk would not absorb water. They gravely misjudge the aubretia who think these things. For those petals are fastened as with hooks of steel, and the stalks have an efficiency which their appearance belies. I have picked the most delicate-looking aubretias side by side with other flowers that seemed far more sturdy. The aubretias were always the last to die.

Of saxifrages there are many, but the very earliest I know, which comes into bloom in February, is the *Saxifraga grisebachii*. It is not always very easy to get. Nurserymen have an awful habit of writing to say that 'Owing to the recent troubles in Turkey, our stock of this item has not been replenished.' Or they say 'In view of the national situation, this item has, unfortunately, been destroyed by mildew.' However, if you persevere you will be able to get some plants.

You will be well rewarded for your trouble, because this saxifrage will light its pale pink torch before the winter days are done, and soon its flame will be reflected in many flickers of answering fire, until one mild spring day the whole rock garden seems to burst into a dazzling blaze. However, you have to exercise a great deal of tact with the *Saxifraga grise-bachii*. It hates damp, and so should be planted fairly high up, where it cannot be dribbled on. It is also wise, during very wet seasons, to put a sheet of glass over it. Some people seem to think that this is a lot of trouble, but personally I think it is great fun . . . like making a little house for the flower, in which it can shelter and keep dry and warm. Also, if you put some small pieces of limestone in the soil around it, you will avoid any risk of mildew.

I will not give a long list of plants, because half the fun of making a rock garden lies in the search which one makes through catalogues, choosing flowers without really any knowledge of what they are. It was in this way that I discovered *Calandrina umbellata* . . . one of the perkiest, gaudiest flowers you ever saw. It only comes out in full sunlight, but when it does . . . phew! You have to shade your eyes, it is so bright. It likes a very dry soil, and you can grow it easily from seed. However, you have to be careful that you do not put it near any red rock roses or purple aubretias, because it is a brilliant magenta-crimson, and will fight violently with any other colour within fighting distance. People have a habit of saying airily that 'flower colours never clash!' I should like them to have heard what a certain scarlet geranium of my acquaintance said to a neighbouring fuchsia, last spring. They might then alter their opinion.

CHAPTER X

MIRACLES

§ 1

WHERE were we? In summer or winter? It is difficult to say. We may, however, assume that by now the garden was in running order, that the rock garden had at last been moulded into its permanent shape, and that the hardest spade-work had been done. For some months now there was peace, in which things simply grew, and made delicious smells and looked adorable. One felt like something in a symbolic picture, clad in shorts and resting on a pitchfork at the close of day, with a lot of hollyhocks (out of drawing) in the background.

But the tranquillity of this agreeable interlude was disturbed, from time to time, by the most astonishing happenings. Let me hasten to add that the disturbances were welcome, because the happenings were nearly all of them delightful. And they were so entirely unexpected that they fully deserve to be called miraculous.

Everything is, of course, a miracle. I am a miracle, and so, I must reluctantly allow, are you. But whereas you and I are used to ourselves . . . know exactly how our hair curls and how our hands are shaped . . . the garden miracles are more fresh and exciting. Every gardener has a strange and romantic tale to tell, if you can worm it out of him . . . of blue flowers that came up yellow, or of a white lily that sinned in the night and greeted the dawn with crimson cheeks. In the strong heart of every gardener some wild secret stirs, of seeds that were sown on barren ground and brought forth an hundred fold. And in this class comes the story of my first miracle — the miracle of the vine.

Ah! The vine! One is exalted even by the sound of that word. It is so beautiful . . . so cool and pure. It is like a soft high note blown on a far-off flute. How Poe must have loved writing:

'The viol, the violet and the vine . . . .'

It is like a triple echo of fantastic music, dying away in a sleepy hollow.

The leaves are beautiful too . . . flamboyantly designed with a fine romantic flourish, flushed when the hour comes with a hectic red, as though something of the virtue of the grapes had stained them with their own sweet shame. You may take a thousand vine leaves in your hands and never will you discover a pair which is patterned in the same shade of red, nor decked in the same design. A vine leaf is a fine thing . . . an aristocrat . . . it curls disdainfully on the slender stem . . . flaunts its flushed cheeks to the dying suns of September.

And here, in the grape-clusters, is the whole sting and sweetness of beauty . . . its bloom and its opulence . . . its poison and its dark fire . . . its gentle, self-sufficient grace. There are some flowers and fruits that have beauty of form, or of colour, or of association, but a cluster of grapes has all these beauties, and more. There is a radiance of much remembered poetry about it . . . and a misty promise of happiness to come. Yet even if these things were not so – even if one saw, for the first time, the heavy purple fruit hanging sudden against the white sky – one would be amazed by the discovery of a new glory.

I cannot honestly say that I ever saw any 'heavy purple fruit hanging,' etc. etc. But I certainly saw something. And I saw it very suddenly, on a thundery morning in August, when the skies were grey-white, as though they were scared of the wild spirits which leapt behind their sober curtains.

§ 11

My father called to me from the garden.

'Here! Come out and look at this!'

There was a note of urgency in his voice. I threw away the book I was reading, and hurried out. My father was standing in the little arbour which leads into the Secret Garden. I went to him, and looked.

I do not know if one's heart ever really stands still, but mine at that moment stood as still as it is ever likely to do, until it stops for ever.

For there, underneath a tangle of ivy, sweet-brier, honeysuckle and jasmine, was a little bunch of grapes. True, the grapes were green and not much larger than peas. But the bunch was perfectly formed, and it hung its head delicately, as though it were diffident that it had been discovered.

'Grapes!' I whispered.

'And how they're alive at all, beats me,' observed my father.

He had every reason to be surprised. The very survival of this vine was a miracle. For its roots were mixed up with those of a rank and greedy laurel. Its stem was being throttled and eaten by a rapacious ivy. Its slender branches were buried, tangled, and overcast by a thick roof of many creepers. Hardly a leaf of that vine can ever have seen the sun. Why, there was even a flourishing elm tree, high above the thicket, casting so thick a shadow that the sturdiest of the creepers had grown pale and anæmic.

Add to all these things the fact that we had suffered the worst summer within living memory . . . a summer of endless rain and biting winds. . . .

Yet, in the cold and the darkness, in the face of fierce competition, the little vine had produced a bunch of grapes. If that is not a miracle, I should like to know what is.

§ III

We took the vine under our care from that day. I was for building a little tent round it, or sheltering it with an umbrella, or . . . if these pleasing devices proved impracticable . . . for procuring a small glass bulb, and pushing the grapes inside it, so that they would have their own house, and would be able to feel that somebody was taking an interest in them.

However, my father intervened. One can't be

whimsical for long, when my father is about . . . a fact for which the reader should be duly grateful, or I would come to every chapter trailing clouds of whimsicality. He cast great scorn and derision on my suggestions for tents, umbrellas and bulbs, and said that the first thing the poor vine needed was a little air.

We proceeded to give it air. With shears and clippers and scissors . . . (for now the whole household was gathered about the rescue of the vine, and every available instrument was in use) . . . we hacked away at the encroaching creepers. The gardener dealt with the brier. My mother sliced off little bits of jasmine, rather regretfully, for my mother is not a born slicer. My father hacked grimly at the ivy. I shinned up the elm and tore off huge branches in a frenzy. At least . . . the branches seemed huge, in that enchanted moment.

Light and air flooded in. I could swear that I saw a swelling in those tiny, pallid globes — a deepening of the bloom about them. And we discovered many other clusters, hanging coyly in the gloom that we were turning so quickly into light. It was really like rescuing prisoners from the Bastille. As each thick and sullen parasitic branch was torn away one had a sense of a prison door opening . . . a gust of fœtid air in one's nostrils . . . and through the strange silence the thin, querulous plaint of the condemned.

Well . . . the work was done. The last creeper was torn away. Fastidiously, and with a sad little sigh, my mother clipped the last leaf that was shading from the grape-cluster the strange rays of the agitated August sun. And then, more than ever, we saw the miracle of the whole thing.

For the stem of the vine was diseased . . . pitted and pock-marked by the horrible hold of the ivy. The leaves drooped from the long assaults of the cloying brier. There was a fœtid atmosphere over this brave plant. And yet. . . .

My father brought us all down to earth. His gruff voice broke the silence. He said:

'Of course, it's the pigs'-wash. That's what it is. The pigs'-wash.'

I gazed, with ill-concealed distaste, at this parent of mine. Here he was, in this sacred moment, which was really Biblical in its simplicity, profaning the air with filthy words like 'pigs'-wash.' Moreover, he went on:

'No air. No sun. Nothing. Therefore there must be some explanation. The only explanation lies in the roots. The roots have probably stretched down into the stream on the other side of the hedge. That stream's always being polluted by the pigs'-wash that comes down from the farm. Damned insanitary. I always told you it ought to be filled in.'

Whereupon, he left his shears on the grass and went into the house to have a glass of beer. I remained, staring at the grapes.

'Pigs'-wash,' I thought. And shuddered. Then, I realized that I was being silly. For do not all lovely things spring from dirt? Is not dung the ultimate essential of poetry? Filth and the fine frenzies are linked by more than mere alliteration. Thus, in this mood of sensuous worship, I kissed the grapes, and bade them good-bye. And I too went in to have a glass of beer.

§ I V

The winter passed. Spring. Summer. And next summer the grapes came to harvest. The vine responded to the affection that was lavished on it.

Affection, indeed, it had in plenty. Our first task had been to whiten the stem of the vine, because the surrounding bushes were so entangled with it that we were afraid of snipping it by mistake. Then we tackled the laurel roots. A very difficult job, this. And then we dug in quantities of bone manure, to reinforce the tonic of the 'pigs'-wash.'

In the spring, when the tiny flowers were forming, I spread a net of thin muslin over the whole vine to take the worst edge off the late frosts. You would have been surprised to see how effective a shield it made. Frost is a strange, queer thing, fickle, volatile, easily discouraged. It was very greatly discouraged by my muslin. It would waste all its nightly bitterness on the muslin, freezing it stiff and snow-white, while underneath the little grape-flowers bloomed gaily, untouched. You see, I wanted them to have a good start in the race for sunshine when summer came.

They had their start. As the warm days came, so the grapes formed, swelled, flushed, stored their sweet juices, blushed with the delicate bloom of adolescence. There was an awful moment when I found a huge and depraved thrush pushing its hideous beak into one of the grapes. I rushed at the thrush, which winked at me, languidly fluttered away and sat on a branch just out of reach. After that disturbing episode we got a net to keep the birds off.

In September there were sixteen clusters of perfectly formed grapes. They were close-packed, of a deep purple, and of a heavenly bloom (except in those places where one had been unable to resist the temptation of fondling them).

Grapes, grapes, *grapes!* I got a crick in the neck looking up at them. And when we cut the first bunch, and put it on a silver dish, and pressed our teeth into the cool skin so that the juice trickled out . . . when we found that they were sweetly flavoured, with real skins and real pips . . . well I repeat, for the tenth time, it was a miracle.

§ v

The grapes, of course, suggested that they should be made into wine. I have not yet attempted to do so, although the idea is quite practicable. Several bottles of good, strong red wine are to be tasted in a cottage in the village. They were made some five years ago, and though the vine from which they came was much bigger than mine, my own vine would produce at least two bottles.

This leads one to the conception of a dinner composed entirely of things one had grown in one's own garden. It would be, you must admit, the most delightful dinner imaginable . . . to prepare, if not to eat. The wine we have settled. The bread would be rather a bore, but if one sowed the potato patch with corn, it should be possible to make at least one loaf. Salted almonds could be served, for I have several almond trees, and even in wet summers there are always a few which ripen. Hazel nuts there would be in plenty, and vegetables galore.

It would be, of course, a vegetarian dinner. However we could have an omelette. Not that I have a hen. But we could hire a hen for the occasion, so that it could come into the garden for a little while in order to satisfy the requirements about everything being grown on the estate. Then, after it had laid some eggs, it could go away again, because I do not want a lot of animals all over the place. I am sure that hens are charming, but I do not happen to want them. Nor cows. If we *had* to have cream for dinner, I would allow a cow to come in, be milked and depart. But I do not like cows in my fields. People are always telling me that I ought to have cows to eat up the grass, but I will not have them, for several reasons. Firstly because cows do not eat up the grass properly. They leave the thistles and nettles. I do not blame them for this, but merely state it as a fact. Secondly, cows make it impossible to take the dog out. They have a ridiculous and unreasonable hatred of dogs. Thirdly, cows are very untidy in their ways. And I do not like having to glare about the ground to see that I am not approaching a danger-spot. Therefore, if we *had* to have cream, I should let the cow come in for just long enough to be milked on my property, and then, as far as I am concerned, it could go and drown itself.

Thus, you observe, we could have a delicious dinner with wine and bread and omelettes and heaven knows what else, all off the estate. Which would be a miracle indeed. 'Hell, it *would!*' said a rude American, who is sitting near me as I write.

§ v i

We now come to yet another miracle. I refer to the pond. It was mentioned, earlier in the book, as a small stretch of water lying at the foot of the rock garden. So, I suppose it is. However, if you knew as much about it as I did, you would agree that it is a whole collection of astonishing phenomena.

Consider the case of the goldfish. A kind friend pointed out to me that one of the drawbacks to any pond was its habit of producing, every season, enough mosquitoes to sting the entire neighbourhood. He added, however, that if one put fish in the pond, the fish would eat the mosquitoes up, and all would be well. When asked 'what sort of fish?' he said 'any fish.' So I got goldfish, which are really the only fish I know.

I bought twelve tiny good fish at Woolworth's. They looked so pale and feeble. It seemed likely that if any eating was to be done, the mosquitoes would eat the goldfish. But perhaps the goldfish would be able to dive if they saw a particularly huge mosquito approaching. Or perhaps, since they were so small, the mosquitoes would not notice them.

The goldfish were in a cruelly small bowl. They could not swim without bumping into each other. They looked as if they were gasping for breath. I took them up into the country in the train, with a sheet of perforated metal over the top of the bowl. A lot of water came out during the journey, so that there was a perpetual pool at my feet, which caused newcomers in the carriage to stare very haughtily at me.

Dusk was falling when I tramped through the field, bearing the precious bowl. Just before I emptied the fish into the pond I held the bowl aloft. The rays of the dying sun glinted on the glass. In glowing enamels the green trees were mirrored. The sky was an arc of grey crystal. And through it all moved the goldfish, rhythmically, backwards and forwards.

I emptied the bowl into the pond. A quick stream of gold and silver, a few bubbles and a group of rings spreading over the black surface of the water, and then the goldfish disappeared. Completely. Not one could I see, peer as I might. A little resentfully I thought that surely one, at least, might have had the decency to swim to the surface, blow a bubble at me, and say 'we like your pond very much, thank you. Good night.' However, not one did come.

Days went by. Weeks. Months. And still I never saw the goldfish. When the winter came, the pond was often covered with ice two inches thick. I used to go down to the pond, on these occasions, to break the ice, partly in order that the goldfish might have some air, but principally because I think that it is very pleasant to break ice . . . to see the jagged cracks, to take a piece of ice and hurl it on the surface so that it breaks with a million, slippery, delicious tinkles. For I had really given up all hope of the goldfish, in view of their complete disappearance, and the only thing that made me feel they might still be there was my gardener's assurance that if they were dead they would float on top. They showed no signs whatever of any tendency to do that.

Spring came. One day I was walking by the pond when I saw a gleam of gold, I stood very still and held my breath. Another gleam. The goldfish! But what utterly different goldfish . . . large and brilliant and all a-glitter! Nor was this all, for swimming about with the goldfish were quantities of other fish . . . even as I stood there I could count over sixty. And the amusing thing about these fish was that *they were all black.*

On tiptoe I went nearer to the pond to see that I was not deceiving myself. No . . . there they were. They were tiny fish . . . about the size of the goldfish when they had first made their début in the pond . . . and they were as black as your hat. This seemed to me the most peculiar phenomenon. Where had they come from? There was no stream feeding the pond. There was not a trickle of water leading into it. The only water which ever went into that pond came from the sky, and it could not, surely, have rained fish?

The sole explanation was that the black fish were the children of the goldfish.

Yet there was something a little scandalous about this explanation which prevented me from accepting it at once. It seemed incredible that goldfish should have black children. Had a black fish got into the pond, and had something unholy been going on? But where, *where* could the black fish have come from? Had one of the goldfish negro blood in its veins? It all seemed inexplicable. I asked my father and he said he had never heard of anything like it, so that it shows that there really was a problem, because my father seems to have heard of most things to do with animals.

Then, slowly, the mystery cleared up. Or rather, the objects of the mystery began to disappear. For one by one the little black fish began to turn gold! It was like a fairy story. At first there was a bronzed gleam on two or three of the fish. Then one day I noted an authentic speck of gold. Soon after that half the fish in the pond were piebald, while about twenty had shed all trace of black, and were going about in coats as brilliant as the original goldfish. To-day there are several hundred beautiful glittering creatures, who disport themselves with the utmost grace, and do not flicker a fin however abruptly you come upon them.

§VII

Of course, one could go on like this *ad infinitum*. For example, I have only to look out of my window to see a miracle. It is an old, hollow, shredded trunk. Its bark is like rotten black cardboard. Tap it and you hear only a dull, unresilient thud. Were you to throw such stuff on a fire, it would hardly crackle, so far do its dim roots stretch into the dank and musty past.

Yet through this sad and deathly passage there flows a stream of eager life. For this is a jasmine, and high above the father trunk the branches take on a strange green life. Old, old as the jasmine may be, it still spangles the early September days with quivering stars of silver, darts and foams and sheds its sweet spray over my wall on many bright mornings. It is tenuous yet strong, delicate and dainty, but there is steel in its passionately curling branches. Steel, or some magic elixir that conjures up these starry flowers from a source so evidently moribund. It is the mystery of birth in death.

The birth of plants would form a theme for many sermons. My last miracle is concerned with the birth of a rose-geranium. To a professional gardener it will not be a miracle at all, but to many men it may seem as strange as it did, in those days, to me. For the average man's ignorance about the processes of reproduction in plants is far deeper than the average child's ignorance of similar processes in human beings. He seems to imagine that trees are brought in a black bag, and that crocuses fall from the mouths of storks. The only plant with whose genesis he is really familiar is the mistletoe, owing to the somewhat embarrassing ordeal which all mistletoes have to endure before they can establish themselves in life.

Of the mysteries of cuttings and layerings and divisions he knows nothing. It is a great pity. I do not mind sexual ignorance in the adolescent — in fact, I prefer it to the hideous precocity which certain shrill educationists wish to thrust upon the modern young. I think that the actions of sexual intercourse are, by the ordinations of anatomy, essentially grotesque, ugly and indecent. No amount of purple romantic veils can conceal this elementary biological fact. I grow hot and restive when I read novels about heroines who lie down on banks of heather, submit to a long embrace, and then discover to their great surprise, in the following October, that they are about to have a baby. Certain very definite and very ludicrous things have to be done before one has babies. One cannot have them with one eye on the sunset and the other eye on the *Oxford book of English verse.*

Plants do things much more delicately. I did not realize how delicately they did it till the episode of the rose-geranium.

The air was full of bronze whirling leaves, the rooks cawed distractedly, and underneath the great chestnut tree there echoed the perpetual plomp, plomp of nuts falling, splitting open when they hit the road, and sending the polished nuts spinning into the wet grass. I went out into the garden, and stood facing the wind. I was excited. I remember that I was humming the prelude of Cesar Franck's Prelude, Aria and Fugue. It is a grand thing to hum when there is a tang in the air and the sense of a dark cloak soon to be drawn over the world. Then I saw the rose-geranium.

It was shivering. One blossom endured bravely on the end of a stalk. It looked like a little hat . . . the summer hat that some wretched woman might hold on her head if she were caught in a thunderstorm at a garden party. The flower seemed to be appealing to me . . . 'Take me in, take me in . . . the frost is on its way . . . soon it will be here to kill me . . . take me in!'

I bent down. What was one to do? I did not dare to root up the whole plant and put it in a pot. That seemed too drastic a business altogether. Yet something had to be done. The rose-geranium was a lady in distress. One could not pass on and leave her bewailing in the storm, clinging on to her little pink hat with tired green fingers.

Then dimly through my mind floated the word 'cutting.' Why should I not take a cutting of the rose-geranium and put it in the greenhouse for the winter? Well . . . if you are a professional gardener you will be quite justified in asking impatiently 'Why not, indeed? What is all the fuss about . . . a simple geranium cutting? Ridiculous!'

But you must remember that this was my first autumn in the garden. I had never 'taken a cutting' before. And though I had heard that it could be done, was indeed done on a very large scale, the idea, when one came to put it into practice, seemed so fantastic that it made me tremble with apprehension.

Do you not realize that the whole thing is miraculous? It is exactly as though you were to cut off your wife's leg, stick it in the lawn, and be greeted on the following day by an entirely new woman, sprung from the leg, advancing across the lawn to meet you. Surely you would be surprised if, having snipped off your little finger, and pushed it into a flower pot, you were to find a miniature edition of yourself in the flower pot a day later? Even if you were prepared for it, your wife would think the whole thing highly suspicious, and might institute proceedings for divorce.

Yet this phenomenon, which sounds like the wildest fairy-tale when you apply it to human beings, does not arouse the least interest in many gardeners, who yawn as they take off their cuttings and push them into the appointed loam.

I am quite sure that I did not yawn as I cut off the little branch of the rose-geranium. For one thing, I was afraid that the gardener would see me and tell me that I was doing it all wrong. I did not care whether it was wrong or not. I wanted to do it all myself. So I went furtively to the greenhouse, found a pot, filled it with the richest earth I could find, and put it in.

The stem sank into the earth. I pressed it down to make it firm. I gave it a little water. Then I stood and watched it. It did nothing. It merely stood quite still, sweetly green. A faint echo of its scent drifted upwards . . . a scent that made one think of sun-kissed lemons, and roses after rain.

Then I pulled myself together, beetled my brows, squared my shoulders, and like a strong silent man, seized the pot and hid it. And rushed out into the night.

148

On the next day I went down to the greenhouse very early. The rose-geranium was drooping. My heart sank. I said to myself, 'it is ridiculous to imagine that it could be as simple as all that. It *must* be more difficult. One probably has to take the cutting off at a special place on the stem, and put it in a peculiar sort of earth and say *ena mena mina mo* over it till it goes to sleep.' However I gave it some water. It should have every chance.

The day after, the rose-geranium had picked up. My spirits soared. But only for a brief space. For was it not quite possible that its life was only being prolonged artificially by water? Would the leaves not have been just as fresh if the stem had merely been placed in a vase? How could one tell if the plant was really forming root? Only, apparently, by pulling it up to see. This, by superhuman effort, I refrained from doing.

And so for another ten days I remained in an agony of doubt. The watering was continued, and after each drink the little pot was put back in its hiding place behind a box of seedlings. But gradually, as the second week drew to an end, I began to feel more assured. When a whole fortnight had elapsed it seemed almost certain that something really was happening. The plant grew perkier every day and even if it had been in a vase of water its leaves could not have been a fresher green.

It was at the beginning of the third week that I knew. For as I was watering it I suddenly saw a tiny new speck of green protruding from the stem. Awed,

I bent down and scrutinized it. I knew every detail of the rose-geranium, and this was something that had not been there before. A moment's examination proved that it was, beyond doubt, a new shoot. In other words, the plant had taken root!

Well . . . there we are. To-day, I have a dozen flourishing bushy geraniums that have all sprung from the little cutting which was taken years ago. You will tell me that it is all very commonplace. Perhaps. However, for me it is so miraculous that I am going to draw a line, very quickly, at the end of this chapter, before I am tempted to break into blank verse.

CHAPTER XI

THE EDGE OF THE WOOD

§1

IT has been impossible in the last few chapters to keep to any system of chronology. However, we can return to it now, because we are about to enter my wood. And it was not till the third autumn that the first tree of the wood was planted. Till then, there was only an empty field, bounded on one side by the lane, on the other by the garden hedge, and elsewhere by similar fields, flat and placid, dotted with occasional elms and willows.

A word about this field. It was three acres of pasture. I was very proud of it. If you stood in the extreme centre of it, and shut one eye, it looked enormous. One had a sense of owning broad acres, and sweating minions, and delicious things like that. However, one could not spend one's time standing in the middle of a field, shutting one eye. People would think it peculiar. So I decided to do something with it.

Up till the moment I had done nothing with it except to plant it with mushrooms which, as you may remember, did not come up. And so I decided that I would turn it into a wood.

To me all woods are enchanted. I cannot imagine being lonely in them. Nor can I share that strange psychic uneasiness which Algernon Blackwood, in

151

several stories, has drawn from the forest's depths . . .
that curious *malaise* of the spirit which some men feel
when the branches are thick about them, and a
thousand green arms hide the blessing of the sun.
There are those who shiver and throw uneasy glances
behind them when they plunge from the open country
into the narrow, tortuous corridors of the trees . . .
and many will skirt the borders of a wood rather than
enter its dark recesses. But I feel that the trees are
my friends, that I could wander naked among them
without hurt, and sleep unharmed among their sturdy
roots.

Besides, there are so many exciting things to be
grown in a wood. Violets among the cool mosses
at the trees' roots, and spindle, that exquisite shrub
which damascenes the dark November days with
rosy spangles . . . the 'apple-blossom of November,'
it should be called. There are anemones and bluebells for the spring and many brilliant berries for the
autumn. And the whole sense and spirit of a wood is
at once aloof and protective . . . it retreats from you
and yet it shelters too . . . brushing your cheeks with
a sweet caress in spring, laying in autumn a pale,
petalled carpet of fallen leaves at your feet, lacing the
winter skies with an iron grille of frozen arms.

However, though I longed for a wood, for its own
sake, I was actually impelled to begin the planting of
it sooner than I had intended, owing to a chain of
circumstances over which I had no control. The
first circumstance was Mrs. Thyme.

§ 11

One day I received a mysterious telegram from my gardener which caused me to hurry up to the cottage without a moment's delay.

When I arrived, I rushed out into the field and saw that there was every cause for alarm. Just beyond the little iron fence, within a stone's-throw of my bedroom-window, a small plot of ground had been pegged out for building. It transpired that the person who was going to build was Mrs. Thyme, a lady from a neigh-bouring village, who supported herself by the honourable practice of midwifery. And all you could say in Mrs. Thyme's favour was that she would have been a better midwife if she had not endeavoured to emulate Mrs. Gamp, when she was so dispoged.

This was horrible. The field, it is true, was not mine, but I felt that I had a moral right to it. Besides I had hoped to buy it one day. Was it too late? I felt absolutely no moral scruples, because there was mile after mile of similar property in the district which Mrs. Thyme could have bought equally well without plumping herself down on me. I must admit, however, that even if this little piece of land had been the last piece on earth, I should have endeavoured to prevent Mrs. Thyme from securing it. For I knew the sort of place she would build. A three-roomed bungalow with a bright red roof and sanitation which is better imagined than described.

For the next twenty-four hours I worked feverishly. I discovered that Mrs. Thyme had not actually got her contract. It might be possible, said the solicitor who acted for the landowner, to persuade her to go a little farther down the road. 'And, of course,' said the solicitor, 'I fully appreciate the fact that you would probably improve the district more than Mrs. Thyme. Oh, indeed? Did you? Are you? No, I do not know the Prime Minister personally, but if you say it is possible that he may be coming up to stay with you . . . yes, I should be delighted . . . perhaps my wife too? . . . most kind . . .'

You see, in my desperation, I suggested that at any moment I was going to be descended upon by Ramsay MacDonald, Charlie Chaplin, Lord Rothermere and Marlene Dietrich, who would all be enchanted to meet the solicitor, but would undoubtedly view with grave distaste the proximity of Mrs. Thyme. It was therefore arranged that on the following day the solicitor should come out to Allways in person and discuss the whole matter on the spot, with Mrs. Thyme and myself.

§ I I I

I am afraid that when I saw, and smelt, Mrs. Thyme I was seized with an extreme distaste for the lower classes. She was very small, with eyes like a malign ferret, and a thin *toupé* that seemed to be attached to her forehead by suction. She spoke in a low, whining voice.

When I was first introduced to her, in my field, I tried to be very gallant, as though she were some elegant creature whose acquaintance I had long been seeking.

'Ah, Mrs. Thyme!' Even as I said it I wondered how such an astonishing aroma could possibly come from any living creature.

'Huh!' she said.

'I see we're both after the same bit of land, what? Ha! Ha!' I glanced quickly round to see if it could possibly be some very unhealthy pig which was responsible for the aroma. But no. It *must* be Mrs. Thyme. So I took out a handkerchief, and for the remainder of the conversation spoke through it in muffled tones, occasionally turning my head and taking a deep breath.

'It's 'ard luck,' said Mrs. Thyme, 'when a working woman can't buy a little bit o' land.'

'Come, come . . .' said the solicitor, 'you know quite well that I've offered you a dozen similar plots at a reduced rate.'

'Very 'ard luck,' repeated Mrs. Thyme.

Booming through the handkerchief, I enquired. 'What exactly was it about this particular plot that you liked so much?'

'I've got to be near my work, 'aven't I?'

She pronounced the word 'work' with a strange and sinister intonation.

'Now, really,' interposed the solicitor. 'Six of the plots I showed you were a good half mile nearer to your . . . ahem . . .work . . . than this.'

'And supposin' I don't always work in the same place?' she demanded querulously. This was so strange and baffling a question that neither of us could think of an adequate reply.

I removed the handkerchief for a moment, took a deep breath and said, 'But I still don't see why this *particular* plot of land . . .'

'I've took a fancy to it,' observed Mrs. Thyme.

This was really dreadful. For here was a reason with which I entirely sympathized. After all, Mrs. Thyme was entitled to take a fancy to a piece of land just as much as I was. The whole thing was really very difficult. Here she was, standing in the middle of my field, with folded arms, saying that she had taken a fancy to the piece of land, and smelling like nothing on earth. It was too complicated.

The solicitor saved the situation : —

'Nonsense!' he said sharply.

Mrs. Thyme scowled at him. 'It's 'ard luck when a working woman . . .'

'Nonsense!' repeated the solicitor. 'You talk as though you were homeless. You already have a house on the hill over there . . .'

'I don't like that 'ouse no more.'

I regarded Mrs. Thyme with increasing respect. She certainly had the courage of her whims.

'Perhaps not. But at least you've *got* it. You want to build another. You've been offered exactly the same sort of land, with the same hedges, the same trees, the same water, or lack of it . . .'

Mrs. Thyme looked up to the sky. 'That's as may be. But the fact of the matter is, this 'ere gentleman don't want a working woman as a neighbour.'

156

This was so poignantly true, that I almost dropped my handkerchief.

'Working woman!' snapped the solicitor, 'I'm a working man. We're all working! Don't talk to us about working, *if* you please.'

I felt that Mrs. Thyme was being bullied. And in spite of her fierce perfume, I did not want to hurt her feelings.

'Really,' I protested. 'You've got it all wrong. It's nothing to do with you.' I took a deep breath, gulped, and went on. 'I should feel exactly the same if, well, if the Prince of Wales wanted to put up a bungalow there.'

This, unfortunately, had an effect upon Mrs. Thyme, very different from that which I had intended. It appeared to rouse her to a frenzy of resentment.

'Prince of Woiles?' she cried. 'What's the Prince of Woiles want in this village?'

'He doesn't want anything. I was only saying . . .'

' 'Asn't the Prince of Woiles got enough 'ouses of 'is own already?'

'Of course. I merely meant . . .'

'Yus. You *meant*!' Infinite scorn radiated from Mrs. Thyme. 'You *meant*!

She glared at us both. Then she said: 'Very well, gentlemen. If that's the way it is, I'll take my money elsewhere. Yes *sir*. Elsewhere. You can keep your bloody land!'

And then, without further warning or argument, she departed. A skunk-like effluvium lingered after her.

'Quite,' said the solicitor, 'a highly undesirable neighbour.'

'Highly,' I agreed, thinking how very appropriate the word was.

§ I V

However, in spite of the rout of Mrs. Thyme, it is possible that I might not have bought the land, nor planted the wood, but for the international situation.

It was a question of seeking shelter. I wanted somewhere to hide in. Things looked so dreadful everywhere. Whenever I opened the paper I saw that my pitiful little holdings in various industrial shares had slid still further down the slope. Everything seemed to be cracking up. England was unutterably weary, America was in the throes of a nervous breakdown, Germany had consumption, Italy was suffering from delusions of grandeur, Spain was about to be sick, Russia had delirium tremens, and France had an acute attack of hysteria following indigestion. The world seemed vulgar, irrational and dangerous. And so I said to myself, selfishly, 'I will make my wood, and hide while there is yet time.'

There was something very fascinating in this idea. I planned to glower out at the world through the branches. Then, if I saw anybody awful coming along, I would rush behind a tree trunk and pretend not to be there. When the revolution came, the mob would march down my lane, see the wood, and pass by. If they happened to see me, and chase me, I could climb a tree and deliver a polite address on the economic situation, combined with a request that, as they went out, they would not trample on the delphiniums.

My mind was therefore made up. I bought the field. The wood should be planted at once.

§ v

There remained the question of money, because I had a shrewd suspicion that one could not call a whole wood into existence without considerable expense. But here I remembered that in addition to my capacity for writing plays which only small repertory theatres would produce I had a peculiar talent for telling women the truth about themselves . . . a talent which most journalists, if they possess it, seem wary of exercising. In the past I had been wary of exercising it too. With this new passion for the wood, I became less particular.

To my astonishment, my articles were taken seriously. My mail increased to gigantic proportions. I was photographed in countless positions. Rosita Forbes rushed across the desert to reply to me . . . and she did it in prose as bright and sweeping as her charming clothes. Rebecca West — adorable creature — threw a cigarette into the fireplace and offered to marry me in a woman's magazine. She said that ought to cure both of us. Mrs. E. M. Delafield, who is the only living writer with whom I should ever dare to take a trip to Cranford, hurled dizzying insults at me in numerous publications. Miss Clemence Dane put out a small pink tongue at me all over the *Woman's Journal.* I have a shrewd suspicion that all these ladies were really buying woods too. Anyway, they roared at me and gnashed their teeth, and the women of England were greatly entertained by the conflict.

When we had all roared ourselves hoarse, and made a lot of money, and, I suppose, alternately wrecked and saved a great many English homes, I suddenly stopped writing articles because I felt that I now had enough to buy the wood. So I went to the nearest nursery gardens — which are fortunately only ten miles away, and are very large and reputable.

VI

It was a lovely day when I first entered those gardens. A yellow September day that smelt like the rind of a lemon. My heart beat fast with excitement as I drew up at the gate and walked down the empty drive. All around me were flourishing shrubs and trees. In my pocket was a fat wad of notes, kindly supplied by the *Modern Girl* — (the author's universal provider). All that was lacking was somebody to come and take my order.

I wandered about, down empty avenues, through

160

deserted shrubberies. I have since discovered that one always does this when one goes to a nursery garden. Nobody is ever there. However, on this, my first visit, the absence of human life struck me as a little odd. I felt like pulling the branch of a weeping willow and crying 'Miss.' At last, turning a corner, I saw an enormous young man crouched in a peculiar position in a small green bush. I could not help recalling one of the most significant of Lear's limericks, and slightly changing it to suit the situation, I advanced towards him, murmuring:

'There was an old man who said "Hush!
I perceive a young man in this bush!"
When they said, "Is he small?"
He replied, "Not at all!
He is four times as large as the bush!"'

I told the young man that I would like to order a wood, if it pleased him, and it appeared to please him so much that he put his fingers in his mouth and produced an ear-splitting whistle. Instantly, the gardens came to life. It seemed as though managers slid down the trunks of trees and clerks dropped like walnuts from the topmost branches. Eventually from this gathering there detached himself a small man of evident authority, who was the top man of all. We will call him Mr. Honey, because it is very like his real name, and it fits him perfectly.

Mr. Honey talked exclusively in Latin.

The first thing I said to him, after explaining that I wanted to buy a wood, was that I liked 'that big bush with red berries over there.'

'*Crataegus Pyracantha crenulata Yunnanensis,*' crooned Mr. Honey.

I took a deep breath, and was about to reply when Mr. Honey waved his arm to the right and murmured.

'*Ribes sanguineum splendens.*'

This, I felt, was enchanting. One had a sense of being a young disciple walking by the side of his master. Overhead there was the clear enamelled sky, all around were flowers and bushes, exquisitely displayed. And through the still air, as he walked, came the dulcet tones of Mr. Honey, speaking Latin.

'*Cornus mascula alba variegata,*' he observed, diffidently.

I racked my brains for a suitable reply. But all I could think of was '*Et tu, Brute?*' Which is the worst of a classical education.

So I said, very weakly, 'I would have liked to see how big one can put in chestnuts.'

Mr. Honey gave me a wistful smile. '*Cytisus scoparius andreanus,*' he whispered.

However, he showed me the chestnuts. He showed me a great many other things. And here is the bill for the first list of trees which I ever ordered : —

	£	s.	d.
4 Standard Limes	2	10	0
4 Standard Silver Birch	2	10	0
2 Standard Laburnums	1	1	0
2 Standard Mountain Ash	1	1	0
Carried forward	£7	2	0

	£	s	d
Brought forward	7	2	0
2 Standard English Elms	3	3	0
6 Austrian Pines	2	5	0
4 Douglas Fir, Colorado variety	1	0	0
2 Rosa Moyseii		7	0
1 Horse Chestnut	1	1	0
2 Standard cut leaf Birch	1	11	6
2 Standard Walnuts	2	2	0
2 Abico Colorado	1	1	0
6 Nuts Merveille de Boluryller	1	10	0
1 Standard Sycamore		10	0
1 Standard Maple dasycarpum		10	6
1 Standard Thorn Double Crimson		10	6
20 Stakes, Tar Cord & Hessian	1	1	0
Foreman's time preparing and planting		15	0
Bus fare and out of pocket expenses		2	9
Special delivery by road, Calling	1	4	9
1 Bundle and packing		10	6
3 Stakes		3	0
	£26	10	6

It sounds very modest. It was. For, in those days, I had myself well in hand. To-day, it is different. I have a dreadful suspicion that before I have finished with my wood, it will cost me every penny of five hundred pounds.

VII

However, if you know a trick or two, there are ways in which you can fill out your wood with comparatively small expense. I have not yet reached the stage where I can record the exciting progress of the trees from the nursery, down the Great North Road, along the narrow lanes, into my little field. I must first explain the episode of the willows.

I had paid several visits to the nursery, and after each visit I left behind me orders for quantities of trees. In my soberer moments I began to worry about the bill. It would be terrible to have to write more articles about the modern girl. On the other hand, it would be still more terrible to have huge gaps in my wood. So I approached my father . . . as one does, in moments of crisis. My father is as poor as everybody else's father nowadays, but he really does *know* about woods and trees and plants. Which is one of the most irritating things about him.

'I am planting a wood,' I said.

'Humph!' he said.

'It seems to be very expensive,' I observed, 'to plant a wood.'

He looked up from *The Times*, glared at me, and said 'Humph!' again.

'I wondered . . .' and I spoke as casually as possible 'if you could suggest any cheap trees . . . just to fill in . . . or something that grew very quickly . . . perhaps a peculiar sort of acorn?'

My father said 'Humph!' for the third time, and arranged to come up on the following week-end.

I am very glad he came up, because it was through him that I learnt many of the trees' more adorable habits. Up till now I knew practically nothing about trees. I had only old scraps of miscellaneous information. For example I knew that ash buds were black in March. But I knew it not from observation but from Tennyson, and I knew it not from reading Tennyson but from reading Cranford. Do you remember the passage? It occurs in the chapter which is called 'A Visit to an Old Bachelor.' It goes like this : —

We came upon an old cedar tree, which stood at one end of the house.

The cedar spreads his dark green layers of shade.

'Capital term — "layers!" Wonderful man!'

I did not know whether he was speaking to me or not but I put in an assenting 'wonderful.'

He turned sharp round. 'Ay! you may say "wonderful." Why, when I saw the review of his poems in Blackwood, I set off within an hour, and walked seven miles to Misselton (for the horses were not in the way) and ordered them. Now, what colour are ashbuds in March?'

Is the man going mad? thought I. He is very like Don Quixote.

'What colour are they, I say?' repeated he vehemently.

'I am sure I don't know, sir,' said I, with the meekness of ignorance.

'I knew you didn't. No more did I — an old fool that I am! — till this young man comes and tells me. Black as ashbuds in March. And I've lived all my life in the country;

165

more shame for me not to know. Black: they are jet-black madam.' And he went on again, swinging along to the music of some rhyme he had got hold of.

So now, whenever I go for a country walk with a friend in March I always lead the footsteps, and the conversation, in the direction of ash buds, thereby gaining an undeserved reputation for literary erudition.

Valuable as is this information, however, it is far from exhaustive. There are a great many things to be learnt about a wood that have nothing whatever to do with ash buds. One of these things was taught me by my father as soon as he arrived. He examined the list of trees I had ordered, and said 'Humph! Let's go and look at this field of yours.'

In the field he tramped about, making hissing noises. Then he turned to me and said : —

'Why aren't you having any willows?'

I was unaware that I was not having any willows. So I said 'I'm not very fond of willows.'

'What d'you mean . . . not very fond of willows?'

I did not really mean anything at all. 'I don't think they'd do very well here,' I suggested.

'Do very well? *Do* very well?' He snorted and waved his stick in the direction of the neighbouring fields.

I looked where he was pointing. Dotted all over the fields were charming trees with leaves of glistening silver and thick gnarled trunks. I realized that these must be willows. Looking back on it, I find it difficult to believe that I really did not know they were willows. To-day I think that I could tell the name of most

166

trees that grow in the United Kingdom, even if you blindfolded me.

'Oh!' I said.

'Good God!' snorted my father. 'You don't deserve to have a property if you don't even know a willow when you see one. This place was made for willows. You could grow any amount of 'em . . .'

'I'll order some at once.'

'Order them? What d'you want to order them for? All you've got to do is to cut off as many limbs as you want and stick 'em in the ground.'

'Stick them in the ground?'

'Certainly.'

'Do you mean that they'll grow, like that?'

He cast a despairing glance at me. Then he said 'Come on, we'll go and find old W . . . He's got a pond with enough willows round it to set you up for life.'

We found old W . . . and we all set out in the direction of the willow pond. It was a cold, squelchy day, with a whipping wind. My father was in his element. His heart has always been close to the land. A natural current of sympathy seems to spring up, instantly, between him and any agricultural labourer. He knows what to say and when to say it. Screwing in his eye-glass, he looks over a field, and says something terrific about the turnips, and the agricultural labourer gives an admiring grunt and agrees. Or he prods his stick into some apparently innocuous clod, and observes that it is . . . what? I forget the right sort of adjectives. I would give a lot to be able to talk like that. I think it is silly to be amateur about anything when one has an opportunity of learning. But I have not yet learnt about soils and the rotation of crops and all those exciting mysteries. I shall, one day.

When we arrived at the pond my father explained what he wanted.

'You can take 'em off about here,' he said to old W. 'There are a dozen or so wet spots in the field where we ought to be able to let 'em in as big as a foot round.'

'Are you going to drive 'em, sir?'

'No. They'd rot from the day they were planted. I want them let in about eighteen inches, and well rammed. Mind you don't break the small branches off.'

We went to examine the places where the willows had to go. 'Of course, they'll need stakes to prevent 'em getting wind-rocked,' said my father. 'Now, about your charge for this little job . . .'

Whereupon my father and old W., with mutual relish and mutual respect, proceeded to bargain with each other. Having been accustomed to pay anything from a pound upwards, with numerous extras, for each of my trees, I was prepared to hear that I should have to pay at least ten pounds for the twelve willows. My respect for my father was never greater than when he finally settled with old W. to pay a shilling for each willow, with a pint of ale as a *benefice*.

§ V I I I

The bargaining had hardly been completed when a shrill voice from over the hedge announced the presence of Mrs. M.

'Ha! Going for a walk?' she cried, fixing us with an eye of acute enquiry.

My father muttered 'God! I'm off.' He bowed very politely to Mrs. M., beckoned to old W., and the two of them departed abruptly.

'Where is your father going?' asked Mrs. M.

'I don't know. I don't think he's feeling very well.'

Mrs. M. was not deceived by this. 'Nothing serious I hope?' she said sarcastically.

'Oh, no.'

She remained glaring fixedly at me. She was quite determined to find out what we had all been doing at the pond. In normal circumstances I should have been equally determined not to tell her. But to-day I was so excited by the idea of getting twelve willows for twelve shillings that I felt less hostile to Mrs. M. So I told her.

'Old W. is going to give me twelve willows for twelve shillings,' I said.

She pricked up her ears. 'What do you mean?'

I repeated the information, and explained how the willows were going to be planted.

She shook her head. 'Very dangerous,' she said. 'They won't get enough water. Unless, of course you're planting them by the edge of a stream. But as you really haven't *got* a proper stream . . .' she paused, waiting.

'Oh it's not at all dangerous,' I said airily. 'We've often done it. They grow like wild-fire. And they aren't going near my stream — which, by the way, is flooded at the moment. They might get washed away.'

We breathed hostility at each other across the hedge.
'Then where are they going?'

'In my wood.' As I said this I turned slightly away as though the conversation was ended.

'But you haven't got a wood!' cried Mrs. M. There was such an agony of feminine enquiry in her voice that I had not the heart to leave her like that, in mid-air. She would not have slept at night with the mystery of the wood still unsolved. So I turned back again.

'No,' I replied. 'Not yet. I'm planting one.'

'Planting a wood!' She grew quite red in the face. This was indeed news. She licked her lips several times, gulped, and then demanded:

'Where are you planting it?'

I told her.

'*Not* the field with the big elm in it?' There was intense foreboding in Mrs. M's. voice.

'Yes . . . why?'

'Oh dear . . . that's very unfortunate. I'm afraid . . .' She shook her head again. But there was a look of unholy relish in her eye.

'Why? What is the matter with the field?'

'Well . . .' she observed, with a hiss of indrawn breath, 'that was where all the horses and cattle were buried when they had the foot and mouth disease.'

This was such a startling piece of information that I was a little taken aback. However, I pulled myself together.

'When were they buried there?'

'Oh . . . it must have been a good forty years ago.'

'Surely you don't remember that, Mrs. M?'

She smiled acidly. 'No. I do not. But my gardener's uncle remembers it perfectly. Before you bought the field, they were digging a pond and they found a lot of bones.'

'Perhaps Crippen used to live there.' (I am very sorry, but Mrs. M. makes one say those foolish things.)

She projected her rabbit's teeth at me. 'Very likely,' she said.

'Why should it matter if the horses *were* buried in my field?' I demanded. 'I should have thought they'd have made the soil richer.'

'The horses,' intoned Mrs. M. in an infuriatingly superior tone, 'were buried in quantities of lime to destroy the — ahem, to destroy the — ahem . . .'

I could not bear her going on like a gramophone record that has got stuck, so I said, 'To stop them smelling?'

'And,' continued Mrs. M. very hastily, 'the net result of it all will be that your trees will go to root.'

I glared at Mrs. M. with a hatred that I did not attempt to conceal. There she stood, on the other side of the hedge with her rakish hat and her rabbit's teeth, telling me blandly that my trees would 'go to root.' I had not the faintest idea what she meant, but I was quite certain that it was something very unpleasant. Did she mean that my trees would stand on their heads with their roots in the air? Did she mean that my trees would run away? Or come out in obscene shapes? Or make fearful smells? It was too, too cruel of Mrs. M. I hated her. For I knew that she wanted my trees to 'go to root.' I felt that she was cursing them at this very moment.

I bade Mrs. M. a curt good morning.

When I got home, I burst into the sitting room, to find my father in the most comfortable arm-chair, reading *Legends and Traditions of Huntingdonshire*.

'Mrs. M. says my trees will go to root,' I exclaimed, breathlessly.

'What's that?'

I explained about the buried horses. My father listened unmoved.

'Damn fool of a woman,' he said, when I had finished. 'They won't. And if they did, hasn't she ever heard of root-pruning?'

'I'm sure she hasn't.' I spoke with bitter contempt, although I had never heard of root-pruning myself.

'Then what does she want to come round sticking her nose into your field for? Horses buried in lime! Pshaw! Now, if *she'd* been buried in that field, there'd be something to worry about!' And he laughed loudly at his own joke.

All the same there was a slightly perturbed look in his eye. For the next few days he hovered round old W., who was digging holes for the trees. From time to time he would take up bits of earth and examine them. I noticed, too, several letters in his handwriting, standing on the hall table at post-time, addressed to the Board of Agriculture. And when my father begins a correspondence with the Board of Agriculture it may be confidently asserted that at least one tax-payer is getting his money's worth.

172

However, as time went on, Mrs. M. was proved to be a false prophet. For the trees flourished so abundantly that the lime must long ago have been dissolved into the forgiving earth. As for the horses, even their bones had disappeared, and their spirits, let us hope, were grazing peacefully in the Elysian fields.

CHAPTER XII

IN THE WOOD

§ 1

By the middle of November I had ordered about sixty trees. In addition to these, we had the twelve willows, by arrangement with Mr. W. We also had a miscellaneous collection of my own which I had been secreting for months past. This collection included a small green shoot which I had grown in a pot from an orange pip, several peach stones, a rather disgusting-looking sycamore, and a few harsh and repellant trees from Harrod's in pale pink pots that had been saved from a dull Christmas party the year before.

However, all things considered, I felt that we were well on the way to a wood.

Now, I had observed, in the woods through which I have wandered, a regrettable lack of design. True, I desired nothing formal . . . I needed no darkly eloquent avenues of yews nor did I hanker after terraced groves of cypresses. (A lot of good it would have done if I *had* hankered!) But I had certain ideas which may be classified under the general heading of 'significant form.'

By 'significant form,' as applied to my wood, I mean that I did very definitely desire to create, in time, certain vistas that should be æsthetically harmonious.

If you choose to put it bluntly, I suppose that you could say that I wanted to put tall trees behind short ones, and light bushes against dark. But I do not choose to put it as bluntly as that. After all, I am writing this book, and so far, this book has not been at all blunt. It has whispered and rustled, and it will go on whispering and rustling . . . as long as I have anything to do with it.

'Significant form.' Often I have recalled that phrase, as I have stood at the gateway to my field, looking out on to the wood that is still in the making. I have seen a line of trees, and behind it, the grey, ribbed sky. In the foreground a splash of lush grass. Green at one's feet, grey overhead, and in between the green and the grey is the black and silver pattern of the trees. These are the enchanted moments when one can play with Nature as an artist plays with a brush . . . when there is an imaginary pencil in one's hand, with which one traces, against the pale horizon, an ever-changing network of branch and leaf. Here, behind this puny oak, we will plant a poplar . . . a gay, green torch to salute the sun. There, in that space we need the autumnal blaze of sycamores. And as soon as the first tint of colour has come into one's mind, there is an answering blaze from one's whole dormant imagination and the mind's eye is dazzled with fairy flames of elms unborn, of unknown oaks and ghostly maples . . .

§ 11

Let us descend to facts.

When I first began my wood I decided to concentrate on a space about eighty yards square. It sounds absurdly small but you have no idea how many trees such a space will swallow up. The more trees you put in, the larger seem the gaps between them.

I did not want my wood to be square, so I bulged one side of it in and out. People did not seem to get my meaning and asked me if the trees on that side were not a little out of place. I replied, somewhat impatiently, that I wanted the edge of my wood to look like a wave spending itself on the seashore. To which they replied that it did not look at all like that . . . it only looked like a few limes, chestnuts and elms, sticking out a long way from the rest of the trees.

But gradually, as the edge filled up, they caught the idea. To help their blind eyes I filled a can with weed killer and traced a long, very wavy path all through the grass along the wood's edge. (This is a very good way of making a path in a field, in case you have never thought of it.)

To give the effect of spray, I ordered a quantity of double cherries, double almonds, weeping crabs, brooms, and half a dozen of that exquisite shrub, *exochorda grandiflora*, popularly called the Pearl Bush. It is indeed well-named, for the blossoms, on a good specimen, look like ropes of milk-white pearls swaying in the breeze.

Then I sat down and waited. Or rather, I stood up and waited. I have never known a winter pass more slowly. True, I had the excitement of the winter flowers, but even these could not entirely hold my attention. Moreover, I was constantly driven to distraction by the uncanny appearance of Mrs. M., who had a habit of popping up unexpectedly from behind a hedge when I was wandering about stroking the tree trunks and looking for buds.

'Well . . . they're still there!' she would bark at me.

'Yes,' I replied, without encouragement.

'Haven't you finished counting them yet? Ha! Ha! He! He!'

The blackest glances never prevented her from laughing at this dreadful joke, nor did she ever fail to follow it up with:

'Quite a forest, haven't you? Ha! Ha! Ho! Ho!'

I said before that I was convinced that Mrs. M. was a witch, and I was more than ever certain of it now. She was always asking if she might come in my wood, but I would never let her. I was taking no chances.

At last the leaves began to come out. First the golden brown buds of the double cherry unfolded, then the lovely sticky pods of the horse-chestnuts, then the mountain ashes and the maples. Looking back on that first year, I wonder if I shall ever find again the rapture which was aroused by those first pale flowers. Those few hesitant leaves, those sparse and spectral berries! Will the stronger, more lavish fruits of later years ever cause the heart to beat quite so quickly in gratitude and in anxiety?

What had I? So little that you may well laugh at it . . . nor shall I care if you laugh, for you cannot laugh away the memory of my delight. A few pink paper blossoms of the double cherry, some guelder-roses that might have come from a doll's house, one pink horse chestnut flower — yes, only one, but it was at the very top of the tree and it looked very grand — a little spring broom, some summer broom, about three flowers of a mock orange, a few thin threads of mountain ash berries, one or two sprays of holly. In the flower and berry time, that was all.

Nor was there much in the tree line. But only one tree died. That was the big elm which, against the advice of Mr. Honey, I had insisted on having transplanted from the nurseries. It was to have been my king of the forest, but it died. As the spring grew later and later, and gave way to early summer, and as its boughs remained black and leafless, my heart sank within me. I felt like a murderer. It had looked so strong and happy when I had seen it in the nursery garden . . . and now, it was dead. It is a dreadful thing to kill a tree, and often, when I am walking through the little wood, I shy and almost stumble, as though I had run into an unseen trunk, and then I realize I am walking over the grave of the elm that I had killed.

All the willows did wonderfully, much to the disgust of Mrs. M. It was an unhappy spring for her. She made as much capital as she possibly could out of the

Autumn

death of the elm, but even she could not be entirely
blind to the flourishing condition of the other trees.

She therefore made the most of the gaps. There
was nothing at all in the centre of the field. So she
would stare at the blank space, fixedly, and say:

'Quite a sight, isn't it?'

I agreed.

'They'll need thinning out soon, ha! ha! he! he!'

'They will, when I've put in all the things I've
ordered for this autumn.'

She shot me a barbed glance. 'You rich young
authors!'

Then she discovered some of my old articles on the
modern girl. She must have read them in a dentist's
waiting-room, or somewhere like that, for she was
far too mean to buy a magazine for herself. She had a
strange instinct for choosing the one subject of conversation which was likely to irritate, and she realized
that any reference to these articles irritated me.
Therefore, she referred to them on every possible
opportunity.

Popping up over the hedge, she would say:

'What weather!'

'Awful, isn't it?'

'I've just been reading your fascinating article on
"What you would buy your wife." Tell me, do you
really mean all you write?'

'I don't know. Why?'

'Would you really buy your wife a mirror so that she
could see how old she was getting?'

'Whatever put that idea into your head?' I exclaimed. 'A mirror's the last thing I should buy any woman. Mirrors are congenitally incapable of telling the truth.'

Mrs. M. shot out her rabbit's teeth in a fierce grimace. 'But you said . . . .'

'Oh . . . I see. What I said then has nothing to do with it. I've changed my mind.'

'But surely. . . .'

§III

Enough of Mrs. M. It is a shame to taunt her so. Everything seemed to conspire against her. Even the weather. For the first spring which followed the planting of my wood was one of the wettest that England ever knew . . . in fact, nothing could have been wetter, except the summer that succeeded it. Day after day I would rise from my bed, draw the curtains, and gaze out upon the driving rain. Normally, I should have been driven to a frenzy by this weather, but now, I could purse my lips, suppress a shudder, and say to myself, 'Well, it's very good for the trees.'

This, I must observe in passing, is one of the delights of being a gardener. Whatever the weather, however sportive the elements, you can always console yourself by the thought that it is indeed an ill-wind that blows no plant any good. Even when the Great Earthquake came – do you remember it, in the spring of 1931? – I lay in bed, listening to the rattle of ornaments on the mantelpiece, and murmured to myself 'this will make some nice healthy cracks in the new herbaceous border.' When the winter is hard, and loath to depart, you can draw your overcoat tighter about you and gain comfort from the thought that no early fruit blossoms are being tempted to make a premature début. When the sun is bright and yellow there are, obviously, a thousand reasons for rejoicing. And even when the November winds are fierce and chill, you may allow your mind to dwell on the goodness which the ground is receiving from an early and plentiful diet of decaying leaves.

Of course, one does not always exercise this Pullyana optimism. Often one frets, and curses and despairs. But in this summer . . . the first summer of my wood . . . I did indeed gain much consolation, during the long and dreary rains, from the thought of those young roots, so thin, so delicate, so thirsty.

§ I V

It is yet too early to tell of any real woodland enchantments. My wood is still only a glorified plantation. There are many gaps still to fill, when I can afford to fill them. But I have learnt a great many lessons, and before I leave the shelter of these trees in which we have been wandering, I would pass a few of those lessons on to you.

Firstly, do not buy your trees too big. This is a terrible temptation for the amateur. I had many arguments with Mr. Honey about it. I used to see mountain ashes twenty feet high, and spiræas the size of a grown man, and hollies that came up to my shoulder, and I would demand that they should be promptly transplanted to my field. Usually, he managed to dissuade me, but on the few occasions when I won the argument I always lost the tree.

Of course, if you are a Rothschild, and can afford to pay a hundred pounds to transplant half Northamptonshire, clinging in pained surprise to a solitary beech, you are in a different case. But if you are like me, you will get much better value for your money by catching 'em young. Besides, there are many consolations. Even if you cannot look up to towering branches, you can look down to tender shoots. There is something lamb-like and poignantly innocent about the shrill green of a baby walnut tree. And all the very young conifers are fascinating, for you can almost see them grow. Half the fun of a wood is this memory of growth . . . this happy mental catalogue of branches that began as babies, are now reaching manhood, and one day, will shelter you as you creep slowly beneath them towards the dying sun.

Secondly, do not plant your trees too close together. These pieces of advice sound absolutely infantile, I know. You can find them expressed with a far greater wealth of detail in any sixpenny handbook. But I must emphasize my point. For the planter of a wood is so unreasonably impatient. There must be a thicket here, a close cluster there . . . it is all a flurry and a jumble. If you are old, then there is some excuse for this fluster. But if, like me, you have a reasonable expectation of forty years of life, there is no excuse whatever. After all, trees *do* grow. Branches *do* stretch out, and trunks *do* swell. They stretch and swell quite a lot even in five-and-twenty years. And it is then, I calculate, that my wood will be most precious to me.

Thirdly, distrust catalogues. I would not say this about flowers, but I say it most emphatically about trees. The average tree catalogue shows you, as an example of a tulip tree, a specimen that was planted by Queen Anne in Kew Gardens in 1708, and has been deluged with liquid manure ever since. If you order a tulip tree on the strength of that illustration, you will be bitterly disappointed by the slum-like stalk which is eventually delivered to you, by a sulky carman, wrapped up in sacking . . . (the tree, not the carman). The only sensible way to order trees is to visit your nearest nursery, and see the actual tree you wish to buy. Then there will be no disappointments. Moreover, you should visit the nursery on every month of the year in order to see what is out, what looks well in this month, and what flourishes in your district.

Finally — and this is extremely important, though it may sound frivolous, you should have a couple of cocktails before making your tour of the nursery garden, because a slight drunkenness clears the eye and frees the spirit. If you visit a nursery, entirely sober, you are inclined to linger too long at the entrance, and to hurry over the latter part. Moreover, you will be inclined to haggle, and really it is useless to haggle when you are gardening.

If you have one or two excellent dry martinis, well iced, your visit will be far more satisfactory, not only to yourself but to the proprietor of the nursery. For you will leap from your car, see a divine splash of pink in a far corner, hail the attendant with the cleanest face, and cry: 'I must have a dozen of those!' And then you will dance off down the nearest path, always followed by the clean attendant, and you will swerve, instinctively, towards the lovely coloured gracious things and you will order them without stint. The after effects are terrible, of course, but it pays.

Had I not been slightly intoxicated at the time I should never have ordered my avenue of *viburnum placatum*. I saw this exquisite thing on an evening in June, after several toasts in an old inn. Do you know it? It is a lovely sister of the guelder-rose, which was always called 'the snowball tree' by one's nurse. The guelder-rose is, in itself, a sweet creation . . . it hangs its gay wares in the stiffest breeze, and stretches its lively roots in the hardest soil. But it cannot compare in beauty with the *viburnum placatum*. The *viburnum placatum* is whiter, waxier, and of a far more poignant loveliness.

I first saw it in the gardens of a charming house in Kent. I was walking with Mr. Reginald McKenna, who was telling me a great many depressing things about the economic condition of the country. Since Mr. McKenna was an ex-Chancellor of the Exchequer, I began to feel extremely gloomy. But just as he was reaching the worst part of his peroration, we turned the corner, and lo! the avenue of *viburnum*

186

placatum greeted us, in all its snowy, dancing folly.

Said Mr. McKenna: 'And therefore, if the French peasant continues to secrete gold, if the United States continues to add to its already immensely swollen gold reserves, and if the English people continue to keep their money in the bank rather than put it into circulation for the revival of the home market. . . .'

'What did you say?' I clutched Mr. McKenna's arm.

'I said that if the English people continue to keep their money in the bank. . . .'

'Do you mean we ought to *spend* money?'

'Certainly we ought . . . I have been explaining that to you for the last twenty minutes.' There was a certain coldness in his tone.

'I know. I'm sorry.' I waved my arm. 'All these purple rhododendrons, you know. Very distracting, when one is talking economics. But I'm delighted to hear what you told me.'

'Why?'

'Because I'm going to spend every penny I've got on *viburnum placatum*.'

'On *vihumhum plahaha?*' murmured Mr. McKenna, casting an uneasy eye at a large mock-orange. 'Quite. Very beautiful. Now . . . as I was saying. . . .'

And he plunged once more into a brilliant analysis of why the world's economics were being disorganized by the action of the French peasants in hoarding gold. I wish I could remember what he said. But all I can remember is silver branches, swaying in the twilight.

CHAPTER XIII

THE PROFESSOR

§ 1

MEANWHILE, people were coming and going at the cottage.

Mostly, they were young men who arrived in snorting cars, glanced at the garden through the window, and said in one breath 'awfully jolly, d'you weed yourself? Thanks . . . I'd rather have a sherry really.' I happen to like young men like that. Or there were young women who also arrived in snorting cars, looking adorable, glanced at the garden through the window and said, in one breath 'divine, d'you weed yourself? No thanks . . . I'm on a diet.' I happen to like young women like that.

There were also a few old friends, who did not talk about the garden, but just went out into it quietly, and loved it. They showed their love, and also their tact as guests, by spending whole mornings on their knees, pulling up weeds.

There were very few real gardeners, because I have learnt from bitter experience that real gardeners are not very good value on anybody else's garden. They are always thinking of their own. This sort of dialogue takes place:

Myself (showing the herbaceous border): There's nothing like this *cosmos* for September, is there? . . . I mean, for making a real show. . . .

Real Gardener: You *must* see my pink larkspur. Heavenly. Do come down one day. It's only an hour from London.

Myself: I'd love to. These Japanese anemones are rather fine, I always think. I divided them from one root two years ago.

Real Gardener: Yes. And if you come down next week-end you'd be in time for my *coreopsis*.

Myself: My own *coreopsis* is . . . .

Real Gardener: Oh yes . . . I see . . . over there. You really must come. You change at Dorking.

Myself (harshly): All these dahlias were grown from seed.

Real Gardener: Yes . . . yes . . . you *must* see the amazing dahlia I've grown . . . and after you've changed at Dorking it's only twenty minutes, and I can meet you in the car.

I think that gardeners must be like parents. No parent wants to talk about anybody else's child. His own son's adenoids are far more charming to him than any other infant's achievements. And I would rather shake earwigs out of my own dahlias than pick the rarest orchids from the hottest of Sir Philip Sassoon's houses.

Real gardeners, therefore, were few and far between at Allways. They were mostly nice people who came and talked and drank and took the dog out for walks, and were very pleased to go away laden with flowers.

However, in addition to these, there was the Professor. And I really think that he deserves a chapter to himself.

§11

'Why should a wheel be round? Why should it not be square or triangular?' That was one of the first questions he ever asked me, when I went to interview him, years ago, for a Sunday newspaper. I was a raw young journalist at the time, and I felt that I had discovered a gold-mine of copy. If a Professor could ask such astonishing questions about a wheel, what might he not say about 'the modern girl'? Which was the problem chiefly agitating editors at the time.

The Professor, in those days, was more or less my monopoly. He is internationally famous now but he still looks very young. He has a shock of jet black hair, a charming absent-minded smile and the largest spectacles any man ever wore. He is the most spiritual man I know. He is completely indifferent to food, sleep and drink. He has a great contempt for his body . . . and for everybody else's body too. He thinks bodies are crude and hampering things . . . not nearly so pretty nor so clean as a nice engine. His only form of sensuality is smoking. A cigarette is never out of his mouth. As soon as one burns low he lights another from its stump.

I met him at the railway station. He was at the other end of a long crowded platform, but there was no difficulty in locating him, because everybody in the neighbourhood was turning round to stare at him.

Not that he looked odd or eccentric. He was merely indulging his old habit of taking notes. And when anybody takes notes on a crowded railway platform, the British public instantly concludes that he is either a private detective or a lunatic. Especially when, in order to take the note, he stops abruptly, to the great perturbation of porters wheeling barrows, sets down his suit case, sits on it, scribbles a few lines, and then as abruptly rises again.

He sat down for the third time just before he saw me, and wrote something on the back of a cigarette card. Then he rose, greeted me, and handed me a small package.

'Your invention,' he said.

I should explain that we have an arrangement that he invents something for me every time I see him. Since he invents at least ten things a day, this is no strain on him. He does not, of course, give me important inventions, though I am sure that he would do so if I asked him. He gives me the childish ones.

This time it was a cigarette of which the ash would not drop off. 'Last time I drove in this abominable car of yours,' he said, 'I noticed that it bumped so much that the ash dropped all over your waistcoat. The ash of this cigarette will never drop off. Though it might bend slightly, in a high wind.'

It did not even bend. It stuck straight out, all the way. And when I had smoked it as far down as possible, I lifted it up by its other end, like a little sausage. A lovely invention. But a poisonous cigarette.

§ I I I

To walk round the garden with him was a perpetual delight. He always said the unexpected thing.

For example, as we passed under the arch over which my grape vine has clambered, he paused and pointed to a little green bunch of grapes that was basking in the long-delayed sunlight.

'Now I wonder what a bunch of grapes *means*?' he said.

'What it means?'

'Yes. Is a bunch of grapes a cry of joy or a cry of pain? Is that bunch saying "Hooray, look what we've done!" Or is it merely an evidence of pimples?'

'I refuse to allow you to call my grapes pimples.'

'Then we will take it that it is a symbol of joy.'

We looked at a *Rosa Moyseii* . . . one of those lovely Chinese climbers which, in autumn, are hung with masses of long coral seed-pods. He felt one of these pods with his white, bony fingers.

'Is this just a single seed? Or does it contain a whole mass of seeds?'

'Why . . . there are thousands of seeds in it,' I said. 'Rather a waste, when you come to think of it.'

'Waste? *Waste?* Pshaw! What rot!' He flicked the pod impatiently, and frowned at me. 'Who are you, to say that Nature's wasteful? People are always saying it. It's a sort of parrot cry. Well, what conceivable justification have you got for saying it? Just because Nature may produce a thousand seeds in order to grow one plant, have we any right to assume

192

that all the other seeds are wasted? We don't know — we haven't the least idea — what those other seeds are doing; whether they are falling to the ground and fertilizing it for the one chosen seed . . . whether they are affecting the waves of the ether . . .' He straightened himself and glared at me. '*The one thing of which we are certain, in an uncertain universe, is that energy is never lost. It is transformed, but it never disappears.*'

This was the theme of many conversations I had with him. He wanted to know what happened to the energy employed by my dog in running after a rubber ball. He could see absolutely no reason why I should pull up a weed, because a weed was a symbol of energy. When I observed that it needed a great deal of energy to pull up a bunch of docks he said it was I who was wasteful and not Nature.

The whole argument was a little beyond me. But I should like to recall one of his theories which he dreamily formulated that night as we stood in a field, watching the sharp yellow flames that forked up from a bonfire of dry bracken.

'That is what you would call beauty, I suppose,' he said. 'And it worries me. It makes me sad. I don't know why it should make me sad, but perhaps it is because it is a problem which I shall never be able to solve by any scientific formula.'

'You must accept it,' I said feebly, 'for what it is.'

'Yes . . . but the sight of any beauty reminds me that I am a savage. Yes . . . a savage, with clumsy senses . . . blind to a thousand things I should be

N   193

able to see, deaf to a thousand things I should be able to hear. Just look at that fire. It is an example of energy, in a certain stage of development. The form of the energy is altering, but the elements are the same. The elements will be exactly the same when those bright logs are turned into dull grey ashes, and when the flames are dissipated into gas. Yet I shall come along, and shall see the ashes, and I shan't get any sense of beauty, though all around me, in the universe, are the elements which are disporting themselves, so prettily, at this moment. That's what I mean. It is all here, yet I can't see it. As though you had taken a word and jumbled up the letters and made it meaningless. We ought to be able to sort out the letters again and read the message without having to have them arranged for us as though we were children.' He turned away, and added, almost to himself, 'However, I suppose that if we were given a gift like that, we should live in such a state of ecstasy that our idiotic bodies would not stand the strain. . . .'

At breakfast, on the following morning, he was still shaking his head, morosely.

'It's a great problem, this garden of yours,' he said.

'Yes,' I replied. I was wondering if we should have to get in an extra man to scythe the orchard grass.

'A great problem,' repeated the Professor. He sipped his coffee, and shook his head at a long branch of jasmine which trailed right across the window. 'That jasmine, for example.'

'Oh, that only needs trimming.'

'I didn't mean that. I meant, are we right to admire it?'

'Are we . . . *what?*'

'I mean, mayn't we be doing ourselves harm emotionally?'

'Oh, I see.' I realized that he was continuing his argument of the night before. 'Well, I don't think it does me much harm. I think it's a jolly good way to begin the day, looking at jasmine.'

The Professor frowned. 'It's so savage,' he muttered.

'On the contrary. . . .'

'Intensely savage. For why should you admire it any more than you admire a beetroot, or a bruise? Yesterday you went into raptures at the sight of a butterfly perched on a purple dahlia. Why? You wouldn't go into raptures at the sight of the caterpillar the butterfly came from, nor the cabbage that fed it. Why? Because you're a savage.'

'Well, you thought the butterfly was pretty yourself.'

'Because I'm a savage, too.'

He threw away his cigarette, and got up. As we walked into the study, I strolled to the piano and played the opening bars of Bach's Italian Concerto. It seemed to match the hard brilliance of the morning outside.

'There you see!' The Professor pointed an accusing finger at me. 'You're being savage again!'

'What . . . with Bach's Italian Concerto?'

'Certainly. It's all a question of stomach. All music comes from the stomach.'

'Really. . . .'

195

'Listen!' There was that curious vibrating note in his voice which always came when he was very much in earnest. 'Music is rhythm, isn't it? Well, where did man get his sense of rhythm? *From the tides!* Why? Because the tides used to bring him his food. When we were jellyfish — to use a simple expression for life when it was still crawling out of the sea on to dry land — when we were jellyfish, the only thing that mattered to us was the regular ebb and flow of the tides. The tides brought us our dinner. The tides brought us life itself. And it is because of the memory of the tides that we love music. . . .'

A fascinating theory indeed. A theory which demands that you should close your eyes, propel yourself into the past, and wander in imagination down some dim and steaming shore, straining your ears to catch in the sob of primeval waters the faint far echo of a saxophone. . . .

However, the Professor did not allow me to dream about it; he had perceived several dandelions in the crazy pavement outside. And these he proceeded to attack, with regrettable savagery, and with a rusty trowel which Adam himself would have regarded as somewhat out of date.

§ I V

I am not often pleased to see Mrs. M., but when, on the second day of the Professor's visit, she suddenly popped up from behind the hedge, with her rabbit's teeth glistening in the sunlight, I was delighted. For as soon as the Professor saw her, he whipped out his note-book and made a note, gravely regarding her as he did so. And never did a more poignant expression of wild and baffled curiosity pass over any woman's face.

If there is one thing that Mrs. M. cannot bear, it is a secret. By which, of course, I mean a secret which she cannot share. She has her own secrets . . . lots of them . . . which she cuddles close to herself in the most irritating way. When you are walking through her neat and damnably efficient house, you may pause in front of a highly polished silver photograph frame, containing the picture of a pretty girl and ask 'Who's that?' Whereupon Mrs. M. will wag her finger and chortle and say 'Ah!' and refuse to tell you. The only way to worm such secrets out of her is by asserting, with steely calm, that you know the secret. For example, I once found out the name of an enchanting young creature by standing before the photograph and saying, over and over again 'Not a very good picture of Greta Garbo.'

'But it isn't Greta Garbo.'

'The man hasn't caught that wild look in her eyes.'

'But I tell you it isn't Gre. . . .'

'Of course it's Greta Garbo. I know that hat.'

'Really. Considering I. . . .'

'Quite. I expect they were sold out of the other positions. I must really write to Greta about it.'

After a little more of this Mrs. M., in sheer desperation, told me not only the name, but the address, of the lady in question, and also her character. All of the information, unfortunately, was accurate.

This was an unpardonable diversion. But a lazy September sunlight gilds the paper as I write, and the air is heavy with dreams. One would say that there is a drug even in the flickering powder which the bees are stirring, in the purple hearts of the flowers outside my window. It is time to lay aside the pen, and sleep, and then come back, drink a cocktail, and try to catch again some of the bright sparks that still linger in the trail of the Professor.

§ v

It is done. The cocktail, a very mild one, is drunk. But there is a tenderness in this fragrant month that lays one open to the slightest, the most delicate impressions. So that it might just as well have been a strong one.

When one is in this mood, Mrs. M. is more than ever jarring.

I effected the necessary introductions. I laid particular emphasis on the 'Professor,' because I knew that this would arouse Mrs. M. to a frenzy of curiosity. It did.

As we walked round the garden she kept on trying to ask me, in an agitated whisper, what he was a professor of.

'Yes,' I would reply in a loud voice, 'the asters are simply dashed to pieces by the rain.'

'Of course . . . of course,' hurriedly observed Mrs. M., who was not in the least interested in asters. And then, as soon as we were round the corner, she hissed again, 'Is it science?'

To which I replied, with admitted ill-manners
'No. It's a geranium.'

'Really . . . I mean . . . .'

'Ssh!' And I frowned at Mrs. M. as though there
were some fearful secret about the Professor which
must never be divulged. It was all very childish, of
course. But if you knew Mrs. M. you would have
behaved just as badly.

And all the time, the Professor was gravely making
notes.

The climax came when we reached the end of the
herbaceous border in the orchard. A lot of new plants
were flowering for the first time, and Mrs. M., having
been thoroughly thwarted, decided that here, at least,
she could get a little of her own back.

'Oh *dear!*' she cried. 'What a pity you put that
fuchsia next to that mimulus.'

'Why?' I demanded. I knew quite well what she
meant, but Mrs. M. does not inspire agreement. She
meant that the fuchsia was a bright purple while the
mimulus was a very assertive browny-red. The two
flowers destroyed one another. However, I was not
going to allow Mrs. M. to say so. I asked her:

'Don't you think they look nice together?'

'They *scream* at one another.'

'Oh, but I always think you can mix *any* flowers.
Flower colours can't clash.' I have never thought
anything of the sort, but, as previously stated,
one will do anything to disagree with Mrs. M.

What Mrs. M. would have replied I do not know.
For, at this juncture, the Professor again produced

his note-book. Gravely regarding Mrs. M. from under his black eyebrows, he scribbled something, sniffed, and put the book back in his pocket.

This was too much for Mrs. M. She gave a shrill giggle, and said 'Sketching me?'

The Professor blinked. He seemed to be looking straight through her.

Mrs. M. giggled again. 'I suppose I ought to be very flattered,' she continued in tones of mingled alarm and hatred. 'Ever since I came into the garden he's been taking notes of everything I said.'

Silence. She hunched up her shoulders, folded her hands in front of her, and alternately revealed and concealed her rabbit's teeth. She was breathing very heavily all the time.

Then the Professor broke the silence. He spoke with such charm and courtesy that even Mrs. M. was momentarily disarmed. He said 'I beg your pardon. But I have a bad habit of trying to remember things that interest me. You interested me just then.'

'Oh!' said Mrs. M.

'Yes. It is really very simple . . . why you are distressed by those two colours. When the red hits you . . . .'

'*Hits* me?'

'Hits you. . .' repeated the professor . . . 'you are at the same time hit — I use the word literally — by the purple. The wave lengths jangle. It is as though one wave-length were designed like this' — (and he drew a long curve in the air) — 'and the other like this.' He drew a series of short curves.

200

'Your mind asks itself the question "which *is* it? I *will* get one of those vibrations." That is why you dislike those two colours in that border.'

I had my own theory as to why Mrs. M. disliked the two colours, and that was because they happened to be in my border, and not in hers. But I had no opportunity to say so because at this point the Professor stooped down, and lifted up a brick. He held it in his hand and stepped towards Mrs. M.

Mrs. M. in horrified fascination retreated. Was she about to be killed? Or was she — in the words of the Sunday newspapers — on the point of being 'interfered with?'

The Professor settled the problem. 'If I were to drop this brick on your foot . . .' he began.

'*What?*' Mrs. M. retreated still further.

He waved his hand negligently. 'A supposition, merely . . . .'

'I should hope so, indeed!' hissed Mrs. M., with a lightning glance at me, in which she managed to 'register' disgust, excitement, and outraged propriety. She could not register any more emotions because she had to transfer her gaze, very rapidly, to the Professor, to see what he was going to do with the brick.

'I only said "if"' repeated the Professor.

'Quite.' She revealed her rabbit's teeth, icily, for an instant. Then her face set again, like a jelly, while the Professor added:

'You would not say, in such circumstances, that the pain had travelled from my hand to your foot, would you?'

'There's no knowing what I'd say.' And Mrs. M., feeling that she had delivered herself of a salvo, gave an unwilling hiccup of laughter at her own joke.

The Professor blinked. Dreamily he said 'No. You would say that the pain was born when the brick reached your foot. It is the same with light. Light is born when it reaches the object it is to heat or irradiate. You cannot say that "light leaves the sun." It does nothing of the sort. There is no such thing as "light" . . . no such thing, I mean, that you catch in space and bottle, and keep . . . It needs you to bring it into existence.'

Mrs. M.'s jelly face did not quiver. The Professor added:

'Do you realize,' he said, 'that when light reaches you, the result is the same as the smell of an onion?'

Mrs. M.'s jaw dropped. She glared at the Professor for an instant. Then she closed her lips, and turned towards me. In tones of infinite elevation she said:

'I think this is a little beyond me.'

'Which is exactly what it is *not*,' cried the Professor, in tones so extremely sharp that Mrs. M. turned round as though she were a naughty schoolgirl who had been caught drawing peculiar objects on her slate.

'It is very foolish,' he said, 'to think that things are beyond you when they are not. Besides, that is the whole of my simile. As long as the thing that I am talking about, i.e. light, is *beyond* you, it does not exist. It comes to life, if you like the phrase, when it hits you.'

I wish I could recapture the rich texture of his talk, instead of being forced, so sketchily, to weave again a thin and imitative fabric. However, at least the sight of the little trio is still clear-cut in my memory. There was a bush of sweet-brier behind the professor — that was starred with brilliant crimson berries. They seemed to be tangled in his hair. Mrs. M. was standing by a white wall, with the clean blue sky above her. She seemed grotesque in this simple, elemental design. I was bending down, endeavouring to persuade a worm to go away from the root of a pansy.

I felt that the conversation was getting too dangerous so I said in a loud voice: 'This wretched worm's got no sense. It doesn't seem to understand what's required of it.'

'The worm has a great deal more sense than you imagine,' snapped the professor.

'The *worm?*' snorted Mrs. M.

'Oh dear,' I thought, 'they're at it again.' And they were. For the Professor turned on Mrs. M. and said:

'Yes, Mrs. M. The worm feels your footsteps when it is underground far more acutely than you would ever feel the worm.'

Mrs. M. shuffled her feet nervously. They were very large feet. She opened her mouth to reply, but the professor got in before her.

'What do you know about insects? Nothing! That is why you think them stupid. Yet the spider's sense of touch is a miracle. And as for the dung-beetle. . .'

I could not help looking at Mrs. M. when this unelegant creature was mentioned. I am glad I did. For her left nostril shot straight up and stayed there, quivering.

'The beautiful dung-beetle . . .' repeated the professor with something like ecstasy.

'The exquisite dung-beetle . . . why,' he cried '*it* makes provision for its young far more effectively than you would do, Mrs. M.'

'Really,' gasped Mrs. M. 'I fail to see. . . .'

I should explain that the Professor had unwittingly hit Mrs. M. on the raw. Her meanness towards her daughter Elsinore, an amiable anæmic who was learning to play the violin in London, was proverbial in Allways.

'Quite,' observed the Professor. 'You fail to see. And when you do see, you fail to understand.' (In justice to the Professor, who is really the most courteous of men, I should explain that he was not really aware of Mrs. M. as an individual. He was lecturing her as he would have lectured a class of rather tiresome students.)

'Your toe-nails, for example.'

And here I did *not* dare to look at Mrs. M. The crisis had, quite definitely, arrived. One could only pray that nothing very appalling was about to happen. But it did. The Professor's voice went on, rising shrilly in the still air:

'Your toe-nails! Why do not your toe-nails shock you? Do you realize that your toe-nails are extremely shocking? Do you not realize that a few years ago you were scratching roots out of the ground with your toe-nails?'

He ran his hands through his hair. 'Of course . . . I suppose I ought not to be shocked . . . but I am. Illogical of me. Because it's my own paralysing ignorance that makes things seem dreadful . . . my ignorance, I mean, of the universal scheme. . . .'

And it was here that I looked up to find that Mrs. M. had disappeared. I ran quickly after her. The Professor was still talking, quite charmingly, when I returned, twenty minutes later. (Mrs. M. had been on the verge of hysterics and was almost unappeasable.)

The Professor looked up as I approached.

'Oh, there you are,' he said, with a vague smile. 'I was just working out rather an interesting theory. . . .'

I felt a little confused and distrait, so I merely said 'Oh?'

'About food,' continued the Professor, blandly. 'It has always seemed to me very ridiculous that persons in different professions should all subsist on the same diet. Now you are an author; I am an engineer, a chemist, and a lot of other foolish things. Doesn't it strike you that. . . .'

But I cannot remember how he went on. The afternoon had proved a little too exhausting.

§ v i

It was the last day of the Professor's visit. The car was at the door. We wandered round the garden, mutely saying good-bye.

'Let me cut you a nice bunch of roses,' I said. 'Look,

these dark ones are lovely . . . if you take them like this in the bud. . . .'

'No . . . no . . . *please!*' There was a note of urgency in his voice which I had never heard before. I turned round in surprise.

His hands were spread out, as though to protect the flowers. His forehead was wrinkled and agitated. He looked like a frightened little boy. Then, he relaxed. His hands dropped to his side, and a slow, delightful grin spread over his face.

'Don't think me a fool,' he said. 'But I can't bear to have flowers cut.'

'I see.' Idiotically, I felt a little offended. I am always cutting flowers.

'It isn't that I'm trying to be æsthetic or anything damn silly like that. It isn't even that I care very much if the flower is hurt. There's so much pain in the world that one can't make every ache and agony one's own personal business. No . . . I only feel, when I stand over a flower with a pair of scissors that the flower is looking up at me and saying "What a *mug* you are! What a poor, God-forsaken *mug!* Don't you realize I'm living, and you like me, and yet you want to bring about my death? For, the moment I'm cut, I die."'

'Yet some flowers last longer in a vase than in a garden.'

He gripped my arm. He spoke very tensely. And there was a wild wisdom in his words, which can only feebly be transcribed. For he said:

'Yes. But we don't know what happens to the *plant*

when we cut the rose. We don't know the influence
. . . good or evil . . . which that action may have
on the ether, nor on the roots under the earth, nor on
the maggots that lie concealed in the leaves. We
don't know to what extent we are impoverishing
or modifying the quality of the air which we have
robbed of its scent — (and scent is tremendously
important) — we don't know how we have affected
the ether radiations from the warmth of the sun. . . .'

He paused abruptly, and smiled again. 'Don't cut
the flower, please,' he said.

I didn't.

As we wandered back towards the house he summed
up all his arguments, crystallized his philosophy in a
few words:

'You see, I'm trying to get rid of the necessity of the
Mascot.'

'The Mascot?'

'Yes. This is what I mean. Most of us find it
impossible to think of anything without first doing
something to our bodies. If we want to experience
the pleasure of smoking we have to take out a silly
little bundle of dried weeds and set them alight. We
can't merely close our eyes and command the necessary sensations to affect us from the ether. They are
all there, those sensations. But we cannot experience
them without the little Mascot of dried weeds. It
is the same with making love. We cannot cause
the ecstasy to come to us. We have to worship a mascot, in the shape of a body. It is the same with a
rose. . . .'

He got into the car. 'They're all here . . . all your roses. . .' he said, and he tapped his forehead.

And that was the last I saw of him, smiling at me, his head full of roses.

CHAPTER XIV

THE GREENHOUSE

§ 1

I cannot remember the time when my family was not poor. There used to be money, but most of it went in the war, and after my father had sent my brothers and myself to school and to Oxford, there was little else that he could do. We had a house in Devonshire, which has now been turned into an hotel, and the garden there was exquisite . . . with some of the finest trees in the kingdom. But we could only afford one gardener, and it was as much as he could do to keep the grass in order.

'Why don't we have a hothouse, like the G——'s, so that we could grow grapes?' I remember asking my mother, when I was a child. She shook her head and said that hothouses were terribly expensive. I was deeply impressed. The idea grew upon me that a hothouse cost 'thousands and thousands' — that only a millionaire could have one.

Yet, I have a hothouse to-day, and I am not a millionaire.

Here, I pause for a moment's reflection. I seem to be pausing a great deal . . . but then, there is some excuse, for the whole of this book is a wandering through a garden, a lazy pilgrimage. And at this place, I would record the curious fact that childish

o   209

impressions of economics are never obliterated. If a thing was a luxury to a man when he was a child, it remains a luxury all his life.

That is why my little hot-house — though it does not cost nearly as much as the annual subscription to my club — still fills me with faint alarm. I go out on frosty mornings, and see the pale, thin plumes of smoke coming from the chimney, enter it and breathe deeply the temperate fragrant air . . . and I tremble to think of the extravagance of it all. 'This is folly . . . this is reckless squandering . . .' so my subconscious mind tells me. It is to no avail that my conscious mind reassures me, by the simple reflection that the expense of the hot-house for a whole winter is not as great as that of a single dinner at the Savoy. The feeling of alarm remains. I feel as though I had invested in a yacht, with a huge crew, and an appalling bill to foot, every week. All because I was told, years ago, by my mother, that 'hot-houses' were 'terribly expensive.'

Yet, it is worth it. Yes — the little greenhouse, with its small stove, and its single row of pipes, would be worth it, even if its upkeep involved my ruin.

§11

To go to the greenhouse when the weather is wild, to close the door, to stand and listen to the wind outside, to the rain that slashes the frail roof, to see, through the misted glass, the black, storm-tossed branches of distant elms, to take a deep breath, to savour to the full the strange and almost uncanny peace which this frail tenement creates . . . to me this is one of the truest joys which life has given.

There is a sense of escape . . . a sense of sanctuary. Thus, perhaps, felt the fugitives, as they clutched the altar rails when the mob was fierce behind them. For here no harm can come. No bitter wind can assault, no frost can chill. I pray, indeed, that the storm outside may increase, that the wind may rise more strongly, that the rain may turn to sleet, and beat a devilish but impotent tattoo on the crystal roof. All the sweeter, then, is the strange security of the greenhouse.

Listen! There are a thousand blustering echoes, out yonder. There is a straining and a moaning in the wood, and a hissing in the hedge near-by. Like the fitful beat of a cruel lash the rain is dashed against the panes, blurring them for a moment, and then leaving them water-clear, so that one sees through them a glimpse of tortured garden. And always there is the agitated treble of water gushing along the gutters into the bleak barrels below. But really . . . these sounds are nothing . . . they have no part in the scheme of things, as long as one remains in the greenhouse. In the greenhouse there is sanity . . . these sounds are mad delusions, the ravings of a disordered mind. There is a silence in here.

Silence. And yet, not quite silence. For if you hold your breath, and listen, you can hear the plants growing. . . .

DOWN THE GARDEN PATH

§III

When I first came to Allways, I took no great interest in the greenhouse. There were so many things outside it which claimed my attention. And so, on the first year, we did not even light the stove.

It was during the second winter, when I was beginning to grow excited about winter flowers, that the possibilities of the greenhouse began to dawn upon me. From the seedsmen's catalogues I discovered that many summer flowers could be brought to bloom in midwinter if they were sown in autumn, taken into the greenhouse with the first frosts, and kept in a gentle heat throughout the dark months.

And so these initial experiments were conducted with simple, hardy flowers . . . forget-me-nots, schizanthus, nemesia, and sweet-peas. They all did beautifully, except the sweet-peas. The temperature was never allowed to fall below forty. The schizanthus was the first to bloom . . . and I shall never forget the pride with which I transported a bunch of these orchid-like blossoms to London in mid-January. About three weeks later the forget-me-nots were ready. I had sown them in shallow earthenware bowls. They looked bluer than I have ever seen forget-me-nots before. The nemesia was rather late, but it was none the less welcome. The sweet-peas failed completely. I have tried them for three years in succession and have not ever brought more than half a dozen blossoms into flower. Perhaps I maltreat them in some mysterious way. Yet, I do not know how. I sow them in the right soil, at the right time, and carry out the instructions as carefully as an anxious mother giving her child its first dose of cod-liver-oil. But nothing ever happens.

On the third year I began to take the greenhouse seriously. For instance, I got the cyclamen craze. Up till then, I had only experimented in the *cyclamen coum*, the rare and expensive outdoor variety which comes from Turkey and produces its tiny magenta flowers while the snow is still on the ground. I had not tried the large, greenhouse varieties. These I now determined to grow from seed.

If you are a professional gardener, you are entitled to snort with rage, and to throw the book away, saying 'the insolence of it! Daring to write about a simple thing like that, as though it were a miracle, when cyclamen are the simplest things to grow from seed . . . when . . . .'

Very well. I don't care. I still think it is extraordinary. When I look at the cyclamen on my desk, with petals of the palest ivory . . . a cyclamen that looks like a flight of butterflies, frozen for a single, exquisite moment in the white heart of Time . . . then I try to think back from the petal to the bud, from the bud to the curling stem, from the stem to the first, fan-shaped leaf, and from that leaf to the tiny seed. And I cannot realize it. Here, in the folds of the flower, are veins in which runs the cold sweet blood . . . here is a stem that rises swift and proud . . . and a leaf of the most delicate and fanciful creation. In its entirety it is a poem . . . a poem that seems.

somehow, to unite the formal rhythm of the sonnet with the wild scamper of a Francis Thompson ode. . . .

A word of warning, however, must be issued to all who first grow cyclamen from seed. You will read on the packet that the seeds 'germinate' in from four to six weeks. This is a black lie. Of course, you may say that by 'germination', the seedsman implies some dark process which takes place in the bowels of the earth. If so, I suppose the seedsman has an excuse. But *I* mean, by 'germination', something that one can actually see . . . a real cyclamen leaf pushing through the soil. And my own experience, of some three years, has taught me never to expect to see a cyclamen protruding from the earth until at least three, and usually four months after the seed has been sown.

These gay and optimistic forecasts on the seed packets cause one weeks of agony. When I first sowed the cyclamen, I hung over those seed-boxes with fierce intensity as the end of the first month approached. All sorts of things happened in them. Peculiar furry leaves sprang up, put out their tongues at me, and vanished overnight. Were these cyclamen? Hell! Why didn't one know? Stately green spears appeared, looking quite delightful, but less like cyclamen than anything you have ever seen. Were these, however, cyclamen? And if not, ought one to pull them up? Double Hell! Why wasn't there somebody to tell one?

At the end of the sixth week, when the boxes contained a dazzling variety of sprouts, I was in despair.

I was grateful, of course, to the sprouts. It was very nice of them to come up. But since none of them could possibly pretend to be cyclamen, my gratitude was not entirely unalloyed.

At the end of the tenth week, I passed by the boxes with a faint sneer. I tried to auto-suggest myself into a hatred for all cyclamen. 'Rather vulgar plants,' I muttered to myself. 'Too obvious. They make one think of bows and ribbons and fearful lattice-work pots. And hot hotel-lounges. And tiresome women who live in flats with electric stoves and indigestion and a Pekinese snoring in the scullery.'

And then . . . on a dank, despairing day, when the whole world was watery and chill, when the dawn was listless and the dusk came with sombre, shuffling feet, like an undertaker who arrives before the last breath has fled . . . I went out, in the fading light, and there, in the seed-boxes, I found that the cyclamen had begun to live. Through the dark earth, a dozen leaves, tiny but strong, had pressed. Oh . . . these were cyclamen, without any doubt . . . they held themselves sturdily against the fawning weeds . . . there was a fine flourish about them, which set them apart from the rank usurpers of their place. And as I bent over them, they regarded me gravely, as though they were saying, 'Well? Weren't we worth waiting for?'

§IV

After the cyclamen, I fell under the spell of the wild gipsy-like beauty of the cineraria. For they are the colour of gipsies' scarves, these flamboyant blossoms, and there is a gleam in their centres which is like the sun in a gipsy's eyes. I did not know how lovely cinerarias could be, *en masse*, till I saw them growing out of doors in Malta. It was April. I had run away from England to try to get a little sunshine, and had made the fatal mistake of imagining that the farther south one went the sunnier it would be. Finding no sun on the Riviera, I went to Algiers, which was like Manchester in November, with muddy streets through which extremely distasteful Arabs trailed vile rags. I stayed in Algiers one day and took ship to Sicily. We called at Malta *en route*. At last, there was sunshine, but even if there had been none I should not have cared, for it was here that I found the cinerarias, turning the whole hillsides into sheets of flame. I picked some of the dead blossoms for their seed, and carried it back to England. It 'took' beautifully, so that my own flowers in the following year cost me nothing. And their colour seemed all the gayer because they had come from no packet, but from the hot, fragrant beds of a southern garden.

A word about this habit of bringing seeds and plants from abroad. When the experiment succeeds, one is enchanted, but my own experience has been rather bitter in this respect. In Sicily, for example, I rooted up quantities of charming little plants from the brown hillsides . . . rock roses, flax, anemones, wild cyclamen, a purple burrage, and some curious pale yellow daisies. I could hardly wait for the time to come when I should plant them, with prayers for their safety, in the cool English earth. But before that time did come there were many tribulations to be endured.

Those plants made one long agony of the journey home. I had tried to wash the roots clean, but it would seem that they had a capacity for producing mud from their own insides, and a marked preference for my dress-shirts as a place to deposit it. I endeavoured, for a short time, to carry them in a jam jar filled with water, but soon abandoned this ruse, because it led to several minor riots at railway stations. Fond mothers, imagining that the jam jars contained fish, snails or even lizards, loudly demanded that I should exhibit the contents to their infants, and when I refused to do so (muttering that there was nothing in the jam jars, but plants . . . not even a solitary newt . . .), tossed their heads, and pierced me with a look of intense suspicion.

But it was at the custom houses that the worst trouble occurred. One does not feel at one's best when one is awakened in the middle of the night by a large man with a black moustache who discovers a quantity of things like damp cabbage stalks wrapped up in a pair of old pyjamas, and proceeds to dangle them in one's face, asking, in fiery tones, what they *are*. What are they? One does not know. It would be delightful to know what they were. Herbs. Yes. To eat? No . . . *no*! Yet, an abominable official in Switzerland, in order to prove the valour of the Swiss gendarmerie did actually bite through the stalk of an anemone. I hope he had a pain all night.

However, a few of the things survived, in spite of the

heat of the *wagon-lit*, and the teeth of the Swiss. Among them is a pretty little rock rose, of a brilliant orange colour, and a flax of so pale a blue that it seems impossible that it could ever have lived through such arduous adventures.

§v

All this is taking us a very long way from the greenhouse which we can now enter again.

Cyclamen and cineraria . . . it must be admitted that there is nothing very sensational in either of these plants from an exotic point of view. No member of the Horticultural Society is going to bite his beard in envy when he hears that I have grown cyclamen and cineraria under glass. Nor, probably, will anybody send me a medal when they hear that I have two very live mimosas, that glitter like sequins on dark February mornings.

Of course, in this country we do not really know what mimosa can be. Even in the south of France, it does not grow to perfection. You have to go to Australia to see it at its best . . . and there it is indescribably beautiful. Though why the Australians should call it by the ugly name of wattle, I do not understand.

The finest mimosa I ever saw grew in Melba's garden at Coombe, outside Melbourne. It was a good thirty feet high and in September, which is the beginning of the Australian spring, it was so covered with blossom that it looked like an immense gold powder puff. One could stand under it, and gently shake the branches, so that the delicate dust drifted on to one's head, and one enjoyed all the sensations of a blonde . . . whatever they may be. Melba used to sit under the tree and sing the lovely barcarolle of Massenet . . . .

Dans ton cœur dort un clair de lune.

Her voice drifted up, like a thread of silver, into the thickly piled gold of the mimosa . . . all around us was the sweet cloying scent . . . and far, far, away the blue mountains, like brooding spirits on the horizon. Magical moments, indeed, and moments which return to me often in my greenhouse, when my mimosas are in flower.

There are two of them. When I first bought them they were about six inches high. They are now about eight feet, and since they show no signs of ceasing to grow, they rather worry me, for the mimosa is a proud plant and does not like you to bend its head or trail it in unnatural positions. However, time will doubtless discover a solution. Somebody might even give me a bigger greenhouse.

As I write of the mimosa I am reminded of another thing which you really must have in your greenhouse . . . a thing which I have seen in no other greenhouse but mine. This is a small standard laburnum.

Maybe, it is quite common, and if it is, I apologize. My only excuse is that the idea of dwarfing an ordinary laburnum came to me spontaneously. By 'dwarfing' I may give a wrong impression, for no actual surgical operation is necessary. You merely take a baby laburnum tree, from three to five feet high, and put it in a pot. You can prune it to any shape you desire. The restriction of the pot prevents it from making any further growth, but it does not prevent it from flowering very abundantly. In the greenhouse, too, it flowers from four to six weeks earlier than out of doors. It looks very rare and expensive. If you take it up to town, and put it in your drawing-room, people will wonder where you got all your money, and will, it is to be hoped, jump to the conclusion that you are leading an immoral life.

Of azaleas, daphnes, grevilleas, begonias, gloxinias . . . of all the happy families of ferns, of the homely heliotrope and the excitements of early bulbs, one could write indefinitely. I have not space for these things.

However, the tale of one of my little experiments may possibly interest a few readers, if only because it may suggest to them a manner in which they can enjoy similar adventures.

This experiment concerned a common field orchid. I am not sure of its botanical name, but I refer to an orchid which grows very freely in my district. It is normally a deep purple, and the leaves are a glossy green, speckled with chocolate. In the summer, the hedgerows are purple with these orchids. The school children pick great bunches of them, and call them 'flags'.

I had always loved these orchids, and wanted to grow them in my own fields, but they seemed impossible to transplant. I dug up quantities of roots, after the flowering time was over, and put them in precisely the same sort of soil, but there was never a sign of them in the following year. So I decided to see what they would do in the more luxurious accommodation of the greenhouse.

What they did astonished me. They grew to double the size and they began to turn white! I had never seen a white wild orchid before, and it would not be strictly true to say that I have seen one yet. But if the orchids continue to fade at their present rate, they will be snow-white before another couple of years has elapsed. On the first year they were mauve, on the second pale pink, and last year they were white with only a faint pinkish fringe. They continue to increase in size, and their whole appearance suggests that they have long ago forgotten their connection with the open fields, and intend to establish themselves, as aristocrats, in their adopted quarters.

This adventure with the orchid tempts one to speculate on the endless possibilities which are open to any man who takes the trouble to transplant wild flowers and give them shelter. I feel that there must be a thousand tiny flowers blooming, more or less unseen, in the fields and the woods, waiting for somebody to come along to give them a helping hand. Not, of course, that one would wish to treat all, or even a large proportion, of wild flowers in this way. Some flowers are wild by nature and would be as ill at ease in a greenhouse as a farm-labourer in a drawing-room. But there are others which seem to deserve better things than the cold winds and the rough soil which is their portion. Among these I would suggest the little purple vetch, the ragged robin, the scarlet pimpernel and the speedwell.

§ VI

I fear that, as usual, there has been too much speculation and too little hard fact in the last few pages. However, we will try for a few moments to sound more professional, shall we? No, we won't. A greenhouse is too much fun to be treated professionally.

Yet most people do not really extract anything like the full amount of fun from their greenhouses. Consider one very obvious example . . . the question of artificial light. After all, nearly all the chief excitements in the greenhouse occur during the winter. And yet not one man in ten has his greenhouse properly lit, with the result that he is robbed of many enchanting hours which he might spend pottering about under the warm shelter of the glass. The most he usually does is to stumble out to the greenhouse before going to bed, strike a match to see what the temperature is, burn his fingers, and drop the match on the top of some wretched sprout that is just pushing its head above the earth.

You must have a light in your greenhouse if you are going to enjoy it fully. An electric light is best, of course, but if you do not possess that, you can invest in one of those small oil lamps with brilliant reflectors.

I do not advise an electric torch, because I always think an electric torch makes one feel agitated and slightly hysterical while it is burning. I can never forget that the battery is rapidly exhausting itself . . . and I champ my lips, and tell myself that I am about to be plunged into darkness and in financial ruin as well. This is, doubtless, another complex inherited from infancy. For as a child I was always told to be sparing of the big torch that lay on the hall table for late comers, and I can remember many evenings when I kicked my shins against the banisters because I had dutifully contented myself with a mere lightning flash . . . a sudden white streak that showed a scared, white staircase and a glistening, ominous family portrait beyond. . . .

No . . . you will never be content with a torch, if the spell of the greenhouse has enchanted you. For how, in a mere flash, can you judge whether the buds of the schizanthus are opening, how can you scrutinize those delicate shapes, to see whether this tint is only a shadow from your own inflamed imagination? How can you linger over the dark and mysterious boxes where the seeds of the sweet-peas lie hiding, like so many buried caskets, with all the scents of spring about them? How can you touch, with the point of a pencil, or with a stick of straw, the infantile green shoots that spring from so many anonymous patches of earth . . . wondering whether this is a flower or a weed?

A flower . . . or a weed! I do not care whether they *are* weeds, in winter, in the greenhouse, in those little sheltered boxes. It is enough that they are green, that their leaves are like fans, that their stems are of infinite delicacy, with a mist of faint and poignantly adolescent hair, which is gilded by the lamplight. Into my mind there drifts the old tag about holding infinity in the palm of one's hand and seeing the earth in a grain of sand . . . it is a tag so old that I can never remember it fully, can never recall, even, from whose brain it came. Yet, it is a tag too apposite to ignore. For here, as one bends over the boxes, and sees the teeming life in them . . . the weed like a spear, the weed like an arrow, the weed like an outstretched hand, and, occasionally, with any luck, the authentic sprout of some seed which one has actually sown, one realizes the rich vitality of a few pounds of earth, and is bewildered by a realization of this world's miraculous and teeming energy.

§ VII

A greenhouse has very definite likes and dislikes. I am quite certain that mine disliked Mrs. M. *She* has a much bigger greenhouse, which was erected for a very small sum by a local carpenter. Everything grows riotously in it. One has a feeling that the plants are working under a system of sweated labour.

It was a blustering November day when she first visited mine.

'What a nice little greenhouse,' she said. 'How much did you pay for it?'

'I didn't pay anything . . . it was put up by the man who was here before.'

'Oh!' She drew in her breath with a sort of hiss, and clucked her tongue. 'Then I wonder why he put it so near the hedge. Let's see . . . yes the hedge lies south west . . . of course, you get *no* morning sun.'

'On the contrary,' I hissed back, 'We get a blaze of sunshine all day long.'

She merely smiled at me, revealing rabbit's teeth. Then she suddenly darted to the little thermometer which hangs on the wall. 'Only forty-five degrees!' she said.

'Perhaps that's because you left the door open so long.'

'Far too cold for this mimosa. It'll never do. How often is the stove filled up?'

'Every morning and every evening.'

'*No!* Why . . . I only have my stove filled up overnight, and it lasts all the next day, and I *never* fall below fifty, though my greenhouse is twice the size of this. What do you put in your stove?'

'Anthracite.'

Again she clucked her tongue. 'Terribly expensive and quite unnecessary. Why — I put *anything* in mine . . . . it burns absolutely *anything*.'

'Such as old pairs of stays and boots and things?'

She did her rabbit smile again, though with a certain effort.

'Would it burn a body?' I asked.

'What do you mean?'

'I only thought . . . sometimes . . . a peculiar smell round your greenhouse . . .'

'Really . . . I think that is hardly . . .'

'But of course, I was forgetting . . . it must be the brewery.'

Which was really unfair of me. The remark about the brewery cowed her, as I knew it would. For Mrs. M.'s garden has one weakness. It lies in the neighbourhood of a very tiny local brewery. True, it is seldom working, and is really only a glorified barn. True again, her garden is sheltered on all sides by fine belts of trees, and one is usually quite unaware of the presence of this sinister establishment. But sometimes the brewery works overtime, and if, on these occasions, the wind is in the east, an acrid odour intrudes itself, tainting the perfume of the roses, steeping the lavender bushes in a faintly alcoholic essence. When this happens, Mrs. M. hurries her guests indoors, talking somewhat feverishly, and I am sure she longs to bury her visitors' noses in bowls of pot-pourri.

So that it was really unfair of me to remind her of the brewery. But unless I am very much mistaken, I am sure that there will be several occasions on which I shall be forced to remind her of it again.

CHAPTER XV

WOMEN GARDENERS

§ 1

From time to time you may have thought, as we have wandered through the garden together, that the women whom we have met, among its winding paths, are unkindly drawn . . . that they are not really representative of women gardeners. I wonder. Of course, it must be admitted that I have made Mrs. M. into a monster, but then she *is* a monster. (Not that I really dislike her. Actually I have a sneaking affection for Mrs. M. True, she sometimes irritates me to such an extent that I should like to pour earwigs down her back, but she *can* be charming. And I respect her because, say what you will, she is a good gardener.)

Miss Wilkins, the 'toon moose', was also a rather sickly character. In fact, now I come to think of it, Miss Hazlitt is the only really charming woman gardener who has appeared in these pages at all. This is strange, for all my early days bear memories of the finest woman gardener I ever knew or ever shall know — my mother. I wish that she could have played some part in these pages. But though I have a fairly adequate conceit of my own powers of expression, I do not feel worthy to write about her. She is to me like a creed, which one believes but cannot express. The very thought of her makes most other women seem like pale ghosts — plain or coloured — according to one's mood. And so, the first and last and most lovely person who ever taught me to love flowers must go unchronicled.

§ 11

But the others . . . they shall be chronicled, even at the risk of arousing their fury. A word, first, in a comparatively affectionate strain.

Most women — and I do indeed apologize for this — are really too *gentle* to be good gardeners. If the word had not been made so hideous by abuse I should have written 'dainty'. For daintiness is their besetting sin. You cannot be dainty, for example, when you are planting daffodils. It is fatal if you mince about on tip-toe, pushing one bulb behind a laurel bush, popping another into the stump of an old tree, and whisking a third, with a whimsical gesture, into the middle of the lawn.

You may have pretty dreams . . . oh yes . . . dreams of one delicate ivory finger pointing to the stars . . . dreams of a pale and lonely blossom swaying in the engulfing green . . . dreams of the single, supreme daffodil . . . which will sing a solo through the spring. But the dreams do not come true.

No! It needs a man to plant daffodils. An enormous man with bulging muscles, large nostrils, few morals and absolutely no pity. He has to be as callous as a mathematician, as orderly as a sergeant-major,

228

and as cynical as a political agent. He must also have a capacity for wild extravagance. For if you really want your heart to dance with the daffodils you must draw squares, triangles and odd shapes in the soil, you must pack those shapes to the brim, you must put in at least six times as many daffodils as you expect to see, and then — ah then, when April comes, your heart will dance, lightly enough! For you will be gladdened by many gay clusters, that seem to show an airy independence of the mould in which their birth was cast.

§ III

I fear that worse is to come. Shortly you will think me the most unchivalrous brute on earth. But the truth will out. And one of the aspects of the truth about women gardeners is that two women gardeners can seldom be friends.

I have proved this a dozen times. A woman gardener can be the bosom friend of a domestic woman, or a business woman, or a sculptress or — if it comes to that — a lady of the town. But she seems constitutionally incapable of making friends with the woman who has a garden next door.

This, when one comes to think of it, is remarkable. For women, when together, usually attain a certain homogenity of sex. For instance, when they have their babies with them, the air is thick with a crooning adulation of Babyhood in general.

'Was it a woojy-woo-woo?' hisses Mrs. A., concerning the offspring of Mrs. B.

'Did it shoo-shoo on the pom-pom?' ecstatically demands Mrs. B., from the offspring of Mrs. A.

'Did it want to poo-poo? Then it *shall* poo-poo!' And it usually does.

These enquiries are not formulated with any desire, or expectation, of accurate reply. They are merely the fevered (and not unpleasing) ejaculations of the feminine animal in contemplation of its young.

However, the feminine animal, when contemplating the Young of the vegetable world, i.e. when glaring with ill-concealed envy and malice at the Other Woman's herbaceous border, is not nearly so sweet and kind. For example, one hears this sort of dialogue:

Mrs. A: Very stunted, darling, your marigolds!

Mrs. B: They're dwarf, dearest.

Mrs. A: So I see.

Mrs. B (icily): Didn't you *know* the dwarf variety?

Mrs. A (with maddening superiority): Not till I came to tea here.

Mrs. B (laughing mirthlessly): How very funny!

Mrs. A: Yes they are.

Mrs. B: What are?

Mrs. A: Your dwarf marigolds.

Mrs. B (sweetly): Not nearly so funny as yours, darling, after an East wind. I always think they look *so* odd . . . with their heads all knocked off.

Mrs. A (sharply): The wind didn't knock their heads off.

Mrs. B: Then it must have been the cat.

Mrs. A: I haven't got a cat!

Mrs. B: Not got a cat? Oh, but my dear, you *must* get one. Think of your saxifrages!

Mrs. A: Why should I think of my saxifrages?

Mrs. B: Well, the mice. Surely it was mice. Nothing else could have nibbled them like that.

Mrs. A: Nibbled? They aren't nibbled. They're meant to look like that. It's a new sort.

And so on *ad nauseam*.

§ IV

How different was Miss Hazlitt!

I make no excuse for referring to her again, for she taught me something that I want to hand on to you. It is the most enchanting of all outdoor sports — THE WILD FLOWER RACE.

I think . . . no, I am certain . . . that THE WILD FLOWER RACE is the happiest occupation that the world has to offer. It is better than making love, or drinking a good Chambertin, or dancing on a Southern terrace within the sound of the sea. It is better than playing bridge, or listening to Kreisler, or watching people pay money at the box office for one's own play. It is even better than . . . but perhaps it would be wiser to leave that out.

The game is simplicity itself . . . indeed, the title explains it. It is merely a competition to pick a bunch of wild flowers. You are only allowed a single flower of each variety in your bunch, and the one who finds the most flowers wins.

However, it must be played with certain very definite rules. Here are the most important :

Rule 1. The exact moment at which the race finishes must be settled in advance. Thus, if you choose to finish at four o'clock — which is always a good time, because you can count the flowers during tea — you must begin to get near to each other a few minutes before four, and when the hour is reached you must quite definitely stop — yes, even if at five seconds after four you suddenly observe an immense spray of priceless orchids protruding from a bramble bush.

Rule 2. (a) You must also decide at the beginning whether you are going to allow the competitors to count varieties of the same flower. Unless you or your guests are particularly learned, you will probably not be greatly troubled by this problem, because most people are not sharp enough to notice varieties. There are, however, certain flowers which always cause heated arguments at counting time. For instance, there are at least three quite distinct examples of the common dandelion. Experience has taught me that the best rule to make is to allow *all* varieties, but also to advise competitors, in the interests of peace, to endeavour to pick their varieties with some sort of leaf attached, because the leaves are often more obviously different than the flowers.

(b) Again you must settle whether you are going to allow any 'pairing'. This really only arises with prickly plants. In June when the hedges are jew-elled with wild roses, some lazy competitor may say, 'Oh, well, there are such masses of roses — every-body can get one — so don't let's bother.' I usually curl my nostril at such people, and try to think of something mean and awful to say about their past. Decadents, that's what they are, these men who cannot be bothered to pick wild roses, far more decadent than if they lay about on divans in purple pyjamas, inhaling poisonous drugs.

Rule 3. If a competitor, walking on ahead, suddenly discovers a clump of rare flowers, he may pick one of them for his bunch and destroy the others before his rivals discover them. He *may* do this . . . though personally I consider him a low person if he does. This point must be left to the discretion of the com-petitors. (If women are playing, they will destroy everything within reach rather than let you get at it. A woman would eat a whole field of daisies if she thought that she could thereby prevent anybody else from getting at them. However, that is by the way.)

Rule 4. You must have one judge and only one judge. Whenever possible, it is advisable to be the judge yourself. You may wonder why it is necessary to have a judge at all. Play the game, and you will see! You would not believe it possible that people could resort to such frightful subterfuges in order to win. Nor would you be able to imagine the extraordinary things which they claim are flowers. 'Well, I think it's a flower,' says one, holding up a rather feeble stalk of palpable dock seeds. 'Anyway, its very pretty.' Don't think you can quell such creatures by observing, in sweet tones, that it is neither pretty nor a flower. You need authority to deal with a crisis of that nature.

Groundsel is always a stumbling-block on these occasions. Is groundsel a flower? I suppose it is. However, it does not matter, provided that you make a clear rule about it in advance — I mean, as to whether it counts or doesn't.

Rule 5.　When adding up the contents of the bunches, there is only one reliable procedure to be adopted. That is for the judge to place his bunch on the table and extract flowers from it, one by one, re-marking as he does so (in tones as free from malice, anxiety or hatred as possible): 'Has everybody got this?' If everybody has it, then it must be placed, with its duplicates, in a common pool in the centre. Special triumphs of each competitor will then go to form little separate groups which can be counted at the end.

However, the common pool is a very essential part of the game. If you do not have a pool, you will find, towards the end of the game, that the players produce flowers which you feel sure have already been counted. But you will have no means of verifying it.

Those are the main rules to observe. And as I

hinted before, it is the best occupation that has yet been discovered for man on this earth.

For one thing, the WILD FLOWER RACE forms the most exquisite of natural aids to conversation. Good talk is as necessary for the brain as good air for the lungs. Yet usually our conversation is stifled by the stage on which it echoes, just as our lungs are choked by the fœtid air which surrounds us in the haunts of men. How can the fancy have a free flight when men are set about a square table, like dummies, motionless except for their lips? How can the spirit roam in liberty when the body is so grotesquely chained.

Out here, in the open air, one encounters an idea, gives it hostage for a moment . . . and then, it is gone, over the hills and far away, which is the right place for most ideas. The sweet fragrance of the flowers gives to the mind an amiability in which the most fanciful conceptions flower freely. . . . It is impossible to be bored, even by a bore, if a platitude comes in at one ear, it goes out at the other — sent flying by the crowded images of the coloured faces at one's feet. And sometimes, dialogues are born which seem, for the moment, immortal . . . a phrase echoes across a hedge . . . vaguely, deliciously, one accepts it . . . throws it back . . . and here it is once more, with the pollen on it. And one stands still wondering . . . the larks shrilling high above.

'Is passionless friendship a dream merely?'
'Does everything end with Youth?'
'Will it ever be possible to live for the moment?'

235

The voice on the other side of the hedge drifts on. The larks continue their silver choiring. One realizes, for a brief, single, singing moment, that the last question has answered itself . . . here and now.

§ v

A wind blowing through the window ruffles the page, shows me the top of the manuscript, and reminds me that the title of this chapter is Women Gardeners. Perhaps I can save my face, and keep up some pretence of continuity, by giving a practical illustration of how a woman plays the wild flower race.

We will call her the Princess P. She is an example of the fact that women, in all floral matters, resort to low and evil practices. She is beautiful, intelligent, and amazingly amiable. But in this game she proved herself to be almost entirely devoid of all sense of moral responsibility — like all other women with whom I have played it. She will suddenly begin to tell one the most exciting story just as one is passing a rare flowering bush. She will simulate fatigue, giddiness, pretend to have things in her eye, and, worst of all, if she discovers an unusual flower she will ruthlessly destroy all the surrounding flowers in order that she may be possessed of a unique specimen.

This sort of dialogue constantly echoed in our walks:

Myself (coming round a corner and finding Princess crouching in a strange position in the hedge): What are you *doing*?

Princess (with a guilty laugh): Nothing. Look at that r—r—rook. Or is it a c—r—row?

I looked at the rook (which happened to be a starling) and out of the corner of my eye perceived the Princess feverishly uprooting quantities of a small yellow flower, and throwing them over the hedge.

Myself: Oh, how *could* you?
Princess: How could I what?
Myself: Destroy flowers like that!
Princess (indignantly): Destroy them? Who is destroying them?
Myself: Anyway, you needn't bother. It's only a form of Creeping Jenny. And I've had it in my bunch for twenty minutes.

At which she made a disgusted exclamation, and walked on.

However, as the game progressed, all sorts of subtle subterfuges were employed. For example:

Scene.—A broad meadow on a hill. Larks shrilling at incredible heights.
Time. — Twenty minutes later.
Princess (very suddenly indeed): Oh, I am so fatigued!

She sits down with astonishing alacrity and gazes at me. She looks childishly innocent, but I have never seen anybody less fatigued.

Myself: I'm so sorry. But won't you catch cold sitting on the damp grass.
Princess: Oh no. I never catch cold.

Which makes me suspect that she is up to some evil trick. The suspicion is confirmed when, a moment later, she points to a distant corner of the field and cries:

Princess: Oh! Mush . . . r-r-rooms!
Myself: Where?
Princess (vaguely): There!
Myself: I don't see them.
Princess: Oh, but yes . . . quantities . . . delicious . . . I adore mush-r-r-rooms.

I rise to my feet and look. I can see nothing. Suddenly there is a sound of tearing grass behind me. I turn round. The Princess, slightly flushed, is rising to her feet. She says:

Princess: I am no more fatigued. Let us go! Those were toadstools, over there.

In silence, we go on. She has pursed lips, and hums a tune. I, presumably, still register intense suspicion. We reach a stile. She gets over. Before she can protest I rush back into the field, and search for the exact spot where she has been sitting. In a moment I find it. There, in the short grass, are several beautiful wild pansies.

They are squashed almost flat. But they count!

§ VI

The Princess P., however, one forgives, because she commits her crimes with such charm and *élan*. Other women cannot be let off so lightly.

238

WINTER

The main complaint I have to make against them is that they are such appalling liars about their gardens. A woman hates you for criticizing her herbaceous border quite as much as she would hate you for criticizing her profligate son. And just as she always has some excuse to offer for the son—('he's so delicate you know, such an unusual type, too, I always think he ought to be a writer; not, of course, that he has actually written much yet, but what he *has* done is brilliant . . . he told me so himself . . . and very soon I'm quite sure . . . though I do think . . . perhaps . . . some of his friends are just a little . . . still boys will be boys . . .'). So she will make excuses for her weedy, straggly border by saying, 'Of course, you wouldn't *believe* the display we have . . . of course, you've just come at the wrong time . . . last week the Cosmos was a blaze . . . quite a blaze . . . not that we put very much in . . . but I believe the flowers grow well for the people who *love* them . . . I think you said Cosmos didn't do very well with you . . . no? How strange! And of course if you'd only come next month the chrysanthemums . . . yes . . . they look like that because they're a dwarf variety . . . oh, do you? Like them taller? How interesting!'

However, the excuses which women make for their gardens, when you are visiting them, are as nothing to the stories they invent about them when you are a safe hundred miles away. If you sit next to a woman gardener at dinner she will have given you the impression, before the butler has refilled her glass, that though she lives in Surrey, her garden is an Arabian Nights fantasy of beauty. You would think that she could hardly walk through the rose garden because the standards are so prolific with buds, or that she must be sent into a nightly stupor by the fumes of her quite phenomenal wistaria. Everything, according to her account, 'grows like a weed — my dear — really like a weed.'

CHAPTER XVI

AND YET....

§1

ON our little village green, which is only a few yards square, the Terror lurks. It lurks in the shape of six or seven harmless youths with red faces, who stop talking when they hear footsteps approach, turn round, and stare.

They stare, no doubt, amiably enough. They do not make rude remarks, nor giggle, nor throw stones. But that does not make their scrutiny less terrifying. I would rather walk naked into the House of Lords and say 'pish' to the Lord Chancellor than run their gauntlet. I would rather put on tights and stand on my head outside St. Paul's Cathedral. There is nothing more embarrassing than meeting this little village parliament.

Do you remember those lines in the *Ancient Mariner*?

> 'Like one that on a lonesome road
>   Doth walk in fear and dread
> And, having once turn'd round, walks on
>   And turns no more his head;
> Because he knows a frightful fiend
>   Doth close behind him tread.'

It is said that Shelley fainted when first those lines were read to him. Every sympathy is due to Shelley, but surely no fiend behind could be more frightful than the fiend in front . . . i.e. the little group of village youths at the end of the lane, who stop talking when they see one coming. I have known people make detours of a mile or more, over hedges, across ditches, and through wet fields in order to avoid this scrutiny. I do not mind admitting that I have done it myself.

For on these occasions one has the feeling of walking alone in the world before a glittering array of eyes. They are not hostile, they may not even be interested. They are just Eyes. And there is something appalling about a row of Eyes, staring, staring.

The persons whom the Eyes observe are powerless. One is utterly lost. One begins to 'put on the expression' at least a hundred yards away. Chin up, hips swinging, mouth set in a slight smirk. There is a terrible feeling that possibly a button may be undone in some crucial place, but it is far too late to alter it now. What would the eyes do if one suddenly stopped in the road and began to look for undone buttons? They would probably shriek and rush wildly down some steep place to tell their mothers.

Meanwhile one's 'expression' grows. As the boys loom nearer, this expression assumes overpowering proportions. The smirk has now spread, and is quivering violently, in order that it may break at the right moment into a maniacal grin. The eyes are slightly glazed. The nostrils are arched. The feet, which have swollen considerably, make extraordinary dragging noises on the gravel.

All the time the mind is tortured by problems.

Shall one say 'Good morning'? Or pretend not to

244

notice the boys at all? It would be possible, by a supreme effort of nonchalance to turn the head away, just at the critical moment, and say a few bright words to the dog. However, supposing the dog chooses to go on in front, instead of walking behind? It would not then be wise to say a few bright words to an empty road. They would think one was mad. Nor could one, as a brilliant improvisation, shout to the dog to come back; firstly, because the dog would probably not come back, which would make one look an awful fool; secondly, because the words might be choked by anxiety; and thirdly, because, in any case, they would know that one did not really want the dog to come back at all.

At last, it happens. The feet, unwillingly, have propelled the victim to the sacrifice. There is a blurred vision of red faces and listless mouths. Something inside barks:

'Good-morning. Nice Day.'

'Good morning, sir. Yes, sir.'

Like a Robot, with a crimson face, one marches on. In a sort of wild gibber, a few words are spluttered to the dog. Perhaps, as a gesture of bravado, one may even put out a hand to pat the dog, but this subterfuge is not to be recommended, for usually the dog is just too far away to pat, so that the hand is suspended in mid-air, in a grotesque position.

One does not seem to be making any progress. The boys are still only a few yards behind. One seems to be all back. And is not one wobbling in a most peculiar way?

It is even worse, if one is with a woman — especially if she is only a casual acquaintance. Conversation suddenly dwindles. It is evident, by the stricken expression on her face, that she has perceived the boys at the end of the road. She begins to speak absently, in a hushed voice. She tugs at her hat, quickly brushes her skirt, and transfers her stick to her other hand.

She talks more and more wildly. On certain awful occasions I have been with women who have been so terrified that they have been driven to a hideous bravado, so that their voices have risen, in shrill horror to the heavens, regaling the entire village with intimate details of their domestic lives. Usually however, they go on mumbling in a senseless monotone, to which one replies with disjointed and utterly irrelevant rejoinders. Something like this:

She (as we approach the group, speaking in a strangled voice, with eyes on the ground): It will, I expect, won't it?

Myself (equally strangled, swinging stick far too fast): She was, of course.

She: No, I suppose not. Still one never knows.

Myself: That's what I always say. She could have done if she wanted.

She: It couldn't, was it?

Myself: Yes, on the other hand, they are. (Fortissimo) GOOD MORNING.

And then, with trembling knees we walk on. When we reach the haven of the cottage, we both take to drink.

§ 11

The reason I introduced this irrevelance was because I have just been saved from a similar experience
by Miss W. (who has not previously appeared in these
pages). Miss W. is the only person I know who is
completely unembarrassed by the silent scrutiny of the
village boys. But then it is impossible to imagine
Miss W. being embarrassed by anything at all.

Middle-aged, stocky, purple of complexion, her
face glowing with amiability, she tramps about the
lanes humming hymns. She is always dressed in the
shabbiest of tweeds, her hair is a disgrace, and she is
accompanied by two of the most abandoned mongrels
that man has ever seen. Yet she looks, and is, very
evidently, a lady.

When Miss W. approaches the village boys, she
does not look in the least sheepish, and I am quite
certain that she does not feel it. Sometimes she is so
intent upon her hymn-singing that she does not even
notice the boys' presence, so that she marches past
them chanting 'The day-hay thou ga-ha-vest Lor-hord
is ho-ver' through her large purple lips, pausing
in the middle of a verse to whistle to her dog, Spot.
So that occasionally one hears singular observations
of this nature 'The damn you Spot day-hay thou come
here is where the devil is that Lor-hord is good dog
is ho-ver.'

Usually, however, she yells at the boys from the
end of the road, waving her stick, and calling out
affectionate abuse long before she has reached them.

And when she does reach them, ten to one she will leap at the ring-leader and smack him on his behind. I would love to be able to exchange souls with Miss W., if only for an hour.

§ III

All this is leading us back, in a very rambling way, to women gardeners. Soon we shall be able to pay them a few long-delayed compliments. Before we do that, however, we must continue the evidence for the prosecution. Miss W. forms a very good excuse for beginning. For she is the only woman I have ever met who is not beset by two of the worst sins of women gardeners — firstly a sort of wild stinginess, and secondly, a maddening mania for tidiness, at the expense of all design.

Miss W. is not like that. She is poor, and she has only a tiny garden, but it simply bristles with flowers. Every autumn sack-loads of bulbs may be seen arriving at the local station, all addressed to Miss W., and when she goes to collect them there is a gala day at the station. She staggers about with sacks on her back and if a bulb falls out she plays cricket with it, the station-master acting as umpire. On one of these occasions Mrs. M. arrived, all dressed up to catch the train to London. However, before she caught it, she also caught a very well developed Henry Irving daffodil bulb on her left nostril. And she wrote to the manager of the London Midland and Scottish Railway about it.

How Miss W. pays for her bulbs, it is impossible to

say. She cannot have much more than two hundred pounds a year, yet she cannot spend less than ten per cent of that on bulbs alone, and since she is equally extravagant with seeds and shrubs, the total proportion comes to about twenty per cent. One day, if I am very rich, I shall give her a whole cartload of tulips — though without any of the 'parrot' variety, which I cannot abide.

I wish more women were like Miss W. It is not that they refuse to spend money on their gardens, but that they usually spend it so unintelligently. Nine women out of ten go in for quantity, and let the quality take care of itself. You cannot get the average woman to realize that whether she is buying seeds or bulbs or plants, the best is the cheapest. She will hunt for bargains as though she were at a remnant sale. To see a woman in a nurseryman's shop is quite embarrassing — she pays much more attention to the price labels than to the plants themselves.

Of course, there are angelic exceptions, but too often one hears this sort of conversation, as a woman shows her friend round her garden:

'How much did you pay for this Deutzia?'
'Three and six.'

'But, *darling*, Toots Brothers have beauties at two shillings.'

'*No?* I can't believe it.' (Sighing.) 'Still they *did* throw in this euonymous.'

'But angel, it's dead.'

'Oh, yes, it's dead. But it's also free. This Ophelia standard was three and nine.'

'They charged me four and three.'

'*No?* In that case I shall get some more. I hate the colour, but it *is* rather a bargain.'

And so on, *ad infinitum.* I always think that the shady Continental bulb merchants must send their catalogues exclusively to women. They will buy anything, provided it is cheap. Then, when the bulbs arrive, small, mouldy, and obviously inferior in every way, they do not seem to be in the least put out. All they remember is that they have saved a few shillings on the bill.

§IV

The other feminine gardening sin from which I exempted Miss W. was the sin of excessive tidiness. Nobody could possibly accuse her of *that*! At all times of the year, her garden looks like a room which the maid has forgotten to tidy up after a particularly wild cocktail party. However, it is always so full of flowers that one does not care. What does it matter if the nemesia ought to have been pulled up weeks ago? One can hardly see it because the cosmos blazes so brightly. Who cares if the stalks of the madonna lilies are unsightly? They are almost hidden by this brilliant clump of delphiniums. If there are quantities of things which are dead, there are even more things which are alive. I know that Miss W.'s creepers need thinning out, that soon the jasmine will smother the wistaria, and that the honeysuckle will kill the clematis. But of what consequence is that? In Miss W.'s garden it is always a question of the survival of the fittest—a rule which applies even more aptly to the vegetable than to the animal kingdom.

Again, I say, I wish that more women gardeners had Miss W.'s qualities. They are only too often so tiresomely tidy. I speak with a certain heat, because I have suffered from their activities in the garden almost as much as I have suffered in my study. Just as a woman cannot realize that when you are writing a novel, it is necessary to have at least a dozen separate piles of manuscript left in odd parts of the room including the floor, so she refuses to admit that if you want beautiful flowers you frequently have to put up with unsightly patches all over the garden.

Snowdrops . . . for instance. If you want your snowdrops to come up, year after year, you *must* allow the leaves to remain after the flowers have died. They will grow bushy and turn brown . . . one knows that . . . but surely there is something rather lovely in the thought that those leaves are absorbing the sunlight and air, and sending fresh stores of energy to the bulb below, to be stored up and used for the dark days that will come again? Women — I am, of course, writing only of the women I know — do not seem to see things in that light. Their fingers itch to snip off the dead leaves. And if you give them half a chance, they will.

§ v

However, I really must stop this dreadful crowing. The sun shines so brightly outside my window, and the clematis looks so lovely, that for two pins I would draw a pen through all that has gone before, though I do believe that it is true. Oh, that clematis! It is like a silver fountain that springs from a dark green bowl, and hangs on the summer air with a mist of stars.

However, this is no time to talk about the clematis. Nor is it a time to apologize. For I have just remembered the episode of Mrs. M. and the red-hot pokers. And if you are inclined to tell me that some of my opinions on women gardeners are unduly harsh, you may feel that I have some excuse for thinking as I I do, in view of the constant proximity of Mrs. M.

Here, then, is the tale of Mrs. M. and the Red-hot Pokers.

For a long time I had been irritated by Mrs. M.'s airy claim that she grew everything from seed. If you walked through her garden with her you were gradually driven to a frenzy by that monotonous intonation — 'just a penny packet . . . but of course you have to *know* how to do it . . .' 'only a penny packet . . . however, naturally, it needs a certain technique. . . .'

One autumn, this penny packet business drove me to desperation. I had procured, at considerable expense, a collection of red-hot pokers (i.e. *Kniphofia*, synonym Torch Lily). These red-hot pokers had done very badly. When they flowered they did not look even lukewarm. It would have been possible to bear this blow with resignation had I not happened to visit Mrs. M., and to discover in her garden a whole bed of magnificent red-hot pokers.

They blazed with arrogance. They were of a

curiously lurid shade of crimson. Their stems were tall and sturdy. Their leaves were bursting with rude health. They really did look red-hot, and it made me red-hot to look at them.

Mrs. M. was chortling beside me. She had been intoning monotonously the merits of her penny packets. She said:

'Very fine, aren't they?'

I turned to her. 'You don't mean to say that these came out of a penny packet?'

'But certainly,' said Mrs. M. Then — as though she suddenly saw the gates of hell opening before her, in answer to this fearful lie — 'at least, from a *packet*. From seed, I mean. Whether it was a penny, or twopence, or fourpence — I really don't know.'

These last phrases seemed rather funny to me, since I know, from ulterior sources, that Mrs. M. always crosses the halfpennies off her accounts.

However the sense of amusement did not last for long. For when I left her, the red-hot pokers began to proclaim themselves. They stung me to a sullen fury. They seared themselves into my brain. I could not sleep at night because of those red-hot pokers, which pursued me as vehemently as if I had been a religious person in the Middle Ages whipped by the devil's fiery tail.

The weeks passed by. Autumn swept upon us with a whirl of threatening winds. Then one day the winds ceased, and the world was breathless, with that strange hush in which one seems to hear, over the hills, the iron tread of winter, marching on. And again I went to see Mrs. M. I do not know what led me on, but I felt it necessary to see her.

'Yes,' the maid said. Mrs. M. was in the garden. She was somewhere near the iris bed.

'Ah!' I said to myself. 'If she is somewhere near the iris bed, she is also somewhere near the red-hot poker bed.' I walked through the drawing room, out on to the little terrace. As I wandered across the lawn I looked about to try to find something awful to say about her garden. But, as usual, nothing suggested itself. Her Japanese anemones were superb. (They were not any more superb than mine, but they *were* . . . well, I cannot ransack my head for adjectives . . . they were 'superb.' And yet, adjectives come tumbling, naturally, in the wake of those delicate petals . . . for they were still and calm and proud, as though carved of ivory that had flushed to rose . . . they were at once cold and sweet . . . and the heart of every flower was gilt and powdered, as though in *maguillage* for some exquisite and secret fête.)

I averted my gaze from the Japanese anemones (which were superb but not more, however, than has already been stated). A purple flood of Michaelmas daisies swam into my heated vision. Then there were other daisies, tawny and grand, and a quantity of chrysanthemums, and a lot of things which I could not grow at all.

I walked on. The red-hot pokers, of course, would be finished now, so that no maddening blaze would assail me. However their memory was fresh enough to be bitter.

And then, I saw it. I mean, her. Or rather, I
do mean 'it,' for what I saw was only a piece of 'her'
. . . and what I am really trying to say is that Mrs.
M. was presenting to me a substantial portion of
herself which can only be presented when a lady in a
thick tweed skirt is bending down with her head
towards the North while one is approaching from the
South. However, it was not this unconventional
glimpse of Mrs. M. which caused my heart to beat
in sudden rapture. No . . . it was something else . . .
something entirely unsuspected. I felt as Sherlock
Holmes must have felt when, at the end of a particularly fruitless day, he suddenly discovered the finger-
nail of a Siamese twin lying near the body, or something of that nature.

The scene is clearly silhouetted in my memory.
In the background, the yellowing leaves of a chestnut
grove. A thin straight column of mauve smoke
climbing to a sky of steel, indicating that Mrs. M.'s
gardener was burning a bonfire. Bright red berries
glimmering, like sparks, amid dusk of immense, for-
bidding yews. In the foreground a stretch of dark
earth, a bundle of browny-green stalks, that were once
red-hot pokers, the nondescript behind of Mrs. M.,
and —

AND

And a row of large earthenware pots, still earthy
from their recent upheaval, containing, in more than
one instance, the authentic plant of a red-hot poker!

With glazed eyes, I regarded those pots. At first, the
full significance of the occasion did not strike me. It

255

was not till Mrs. M. had turned round, flushed as deep a red as any of her pokers, that I realized the blackness of her sin. For here was Mrs. M., whose lips had paid lying service to the lore of seeds, detected in the contemptible act of removing potted plants from her own border. Plants which she had actually bought in pots! No, more . . . which having bought, she had failed to remove from their pots! A practice which, as you must instantly agree, is akin to such awful things as the White Slave Traffic.

I smacked my lips. This, indeed was a moment to remember. The whole thing was revealed before me. I saw, on one . . . on two, three . . . yes on *four* of the pots, a little label. True, the labels were faded and worn, but I managed, with the unusual clarity of vision which great passion engenders, to detect the Latin name for 'red-hot poker,' and also the name of the firm which supplied them. Then, exaltation was usurped by horror, as the appalling nature of Mrs. M.'s felony burst upon me. It was as though one found a criminal, who for weeks had been violently protesting his innocence, in the very act of dismembering the body.

I looked at Mrs. M. She looked at me. We were frozen in a moment of Time. I tremble to think of the vibrations of hatred, passion, fear, exultation, etc. etc., which must have twanged through the ether, between us, on that occasion.

I said to Mrs. M.:

'Sowing some more red-hot pokers, Mrs. M.?'

She glared.

I glared.

A chestnut fell in the distant grove.

I walked away. We both realized that this was a crisis in our lives. The situation was crazy, unnatural, akin to a wild tale of hobgoblins. But if you are a gardener, you will realize that it was not only credible, but inevitable.

I do not know what to do about it. The discord is still unresolved. Indeed, it clashes so violently that the only immediate solution seems to be that I should marry Mrs. M.

CHAPTER XVII

BOUQUET

§1

I HAVE just got rid of a party whose members, though amiable and charming, caused me great anxiety when they were let loose in the flower-beds. The climax arrived a few nights ago when I discovered that one of my female guests, taking advantage of my absence, had taken upon herself to cut a great many flowers which should not have been cut, to place them in vases in which they should not have been placed, and to arrange them in positions in which they should not have been arranged.

I returned and gazed about me with horror. She entered the room and smiled at me brightly. 'Doesn't the house look lovely?' she exclaimed. I gave her a look, and went out and ate a few worms.

Some women have strangely savage ideas about floral decoration. Hence the household hints that follow.

There are two general principles to remember when arranging flowers. The first is that you must be ruthless with them. Flowers should be hit and punched and strangled into shape. It is useless to drift round the house with a lily in one hand and a geranium in the other, and a Mona Lisa smile on your lips. Nor should you hold the vase absently under the tap, and

258

curve your back into an elegant droop. Nor drop the blossoms into the water, darting back to regard them with poised hands and half closed eyes. You must put on thick leather gloves and jam them in, and curse them under your breath. I will explain more fully later.

The second principle — and this is vital — is that if you want to have flowers looking their best you *must* have an adequate assortment of receptacles for them. Most women have a shelf or two containing a meagre assortment of tall and short glass vases, one or two bowls, and a selection of miscellaneous horrors, whose only conceivable merit is that they hold water. In addition to these there are usually one or two wire cages which fit nothing, and a few hateful glass blocks with holes in them, which look as if they were intended for umbrella stands.

This is a ludicrous state of affairs. There should, of course, be as many sizes, shapes and sorts of vase as there are sizes, shapes and sorts of flower. Since this would mean that one would have to live in a house as large as the Vatican, one must effect a compromise, and get as many as one can. I myself have three very large cupboards stacked with glass and china, and yet I am often unable to find what I want.

§ I I

Let me begin with the arrangement of my beloved winter flowers. It sometimes happens, when the days are exceptionally bitter, in the very frozen heart of winter, that there seems to be nothing in the garden at all. At least, a lazy man will tell you there is nothing. He will walk round the garden once, with his coat up, see a benighted wallflower, its petals stiff with frost, and an early startled snowdrop, and come indoors chafing his hands and cursing.

Now, even if there were only one wallflower and one snowdrop, he could have done quite a lot with those two flowers, if he had used a little ingenuity. But I would hazard a wager that there was a great deal more than that. I live in a comparatively bleak district — I suppose you would call it the Midlands — and I have very little shelter. Yet, on the second year that I had my garden, before I had done much about winter flowers, I picked in the open air, on December 6th, a bunch of flowers containing the following things (I copy the list from my diary):

1. *A rose.* A little frost-weary, but none the less a rose. It was not quite out, but it will come out in water.

2. *A spray of pink larkspur* that had been sheltered by a large stone.

3. *One snowdrop.*

4. *Two or three blooms of purple stock.* The leaves had been blackened with frost, and one or two of the petals were damaged, but I removed the leaves and cut out the bad petals, very carefully, with fine nail-scissors.

5. *A dandelion,* which was growing in a sheltered hedge.

6. One of those little white flowers with thousands of blossoms that grow in the fields in summer. (I have not yet learnt the name.)

7. *Several yellow wallflowers.* They were behind a shrub. Their stalks were coarse and thick, and covered with decayed seedpods, which I removed. The small flowers on top were prim and bright.

8. *Two marigolds.* In exceptionally fine condition.

9. *A late chrysanthemum.*

10. *A spray of blackberries.*

11. *A few pansies.* They had short stalks, but I wired the bottom of the stalk.

12. *A Michaelmas daisy.* This was lying flat on the ground, and its petals were covered with mud. When washed it was perfectly fresh.

13. *Various berries.*

14. *Two violets.*

15. *A yellow daisy.*

That was not a bad bunch for an unsheltered, comparatively neglected garden, in a cold winter. It was, of course, obtained only by a very exhaustive search of every inch of the ground. That, to me, is the delight and the thrill of it. I love, as much as anybody, to go out in spring and to come in again, five minutes later, with armfuls of white lilac. But this search for winter flowers — this foraging in a barren land — with all the elements against you, and darkness so swiftly descending, is to me a keener pleasure.

§ I I I

However, half the flowers in my little list above, would have been neglected or spurned by the average man, because he does not realize what miracles one can work with a little floral surgery when one takes the flowers inside. He does not realize that an almost black rosebud will expand in the warmth, nor that a wallflower's ugly stalk will be hidden if it is placed in the centre of a bouquet. Nor does he realize — and this is most important of all — that even the tiniest bouquet can be magnified to many times its normal size by the aid of mirrors.

This is how you can arrange your minute bouquets of winter flowers. Get a glass merchant to cut three squares of mirror, about one foot by nine inches, and to make brackets of them, using two squares for the sides and one for the base. These brackets can be hung on any corner, or placed on a table, if you wish. There is no need to frame them, or daub them with any sort of paint, for a sheet of plain looking-glass is quite inoffensive — at least, it is as inoffensive as the life it reflects, which may not be saying much.

On these brackets you place your tiny bouquets. And instantly the mirror seems to blaze with colours. Your solitary wallflower has a magic progeny, its gold is multiplied indefinitely. Your spray of larkspur repeats itself in many charming patterns . . . your daisy seems to have a thousand eyes. You can dream over a bouquet like that, into infinite distances.

As a sternly practical hint it should be noted that the effect is heightened if you put the bouquet in a very brightly painted pot. The best pots I ever found for this purpose were in Naples. They were in a grocer's and had marmalade in them. I did not care for the marmalade, but the pots were delicious, because they were a pale cream colour, and were splashed all over with brilliant yellow, blue and crimson flowers. An added advantage of china over glass, in winter bouquets, is that the china conceals the stalks, which will often look thick and ugly owing to the necessity of removing the frost-bitten leaves.

§ I V

I expressed above a certain distaste for the glass umbrella stands which seem to be so popular with many women when they are arranging flowers. I suppose their popularity is partly due to the fact that they save trouble. One can stick anything into them, from a daffodil to a carrot. And as far as I am concerned, the result is much the same. As far as the flower is concerned, too, for the women who use these infernal engines usually push the flower so hard into its hole that the stalk is strangled and cannot absorb any water.

I have invented a way out of this difficulty. It may not be a new idea, but it is, at least, new to me, and I give it for what it is worth. I had long been revolted by the umbrella stands. I had also been revolted by the wire netting, which looked as if it ought to conceal a lurking leg of cold mutton. The wire netting is permissible with a few flowers which have a very heavy foliage, but it is vulgar and hateful with bare stemmed flowers.

'Why not go back to Nature?' I thought. 'Why not

use earth?' And so, I fetched a bowl of coarse green glass, semi-opaque, took it into the garden, and half filled it with earth. Then I brought it back to the house and filled it with water to the brim. It looked horrible, of course — muddy and disgusting — but that did not deter me, for I knew that the dirt would settle in half an hour. So I went and picked a bunch of paper-white narcissi and pushed the stalks in the earth. They stood up perfectly, exactly as they stand in their native fields. And sure enough, in half an hour the water had settled and was crystal clear. Through it shone the stalks of the narcissi, rising from their natural bed, which was bounded by the coarse green glass. I may add that the flowers lasted nearly two days longer than usual.

This idea is, I know, a little one. It cannot be ranked among the major discoveries of mankind. But it has solved many problems for me, and given me many hours of unalloyed delight — which is more than I can say for the invention of the steam engine, and about as much as I can say for the invention of printing. It has made it possible, for example, to enjoy the flawless beauty of a clump of snowdrops in a London flat. I have some shallow bowls of deep blue glass which are perfect for snowdrops. I keep a stock of earth in my London basement, and I am never happier than when I am depositing the earth into the bowls, pouring the water on it, and taking the snowdrops from their tissue paper, setting each ivory bell, with infinite reverence, into its place. A little silver bubble rises through the mud as each stalk is pushed down—a little silver bubble, that bursts and leaves only the brown water. But after half an hour, the water is clear again, and on my mantelpiece the snowdrops gleam. They are silver if you look at them from one side of the room, rose if you look at them from the other. And in certain lights they are tinged with a hectic blue. Why should one want to go out to dinner when one can stay at home with the snow-drops, and enjoy them in solitude? It took a few million years to make a snowdrop. Surely one is justified in spending a few hours in studying the results?

I had not intended these moralizations, but the mere memory of a snowdrop, in these blazing days when I write, is like a white flag challenging me to surrender my self-control.

§V

But now I come to my really great invention, by which I hope to achieve immortality.

I had long been worried by the difficulty of trans-porting certain flowers from the country to London. After every week-end I used to set off with my car so full of flowers that it looked as though it were about to compete in a Nice carnival. By the time I arrived in London some of the flowers were always bruised beyond repair. Most of them survived well enough, but some were in a tragic condition.

The dahlias were the worst. It seemed that the petals of the dahlia were so delicate that the least thing would turn them brown. This saddened me, because

I love dahlias, and in the cottage they used to last for a week.

Then one day, when I was scowling at the dahlia bed, and on the point of accusing the flowers of doing it on purpose, I had a brain wave. Why not get a small sheet, hang it in the car suspended from the roof, and then pass the stalks of the dahlias through it, so that the blossoms rested on the sheet, without touching one another, and the stalks dangled down into the air? The fact that one would look like the old woman who lived in a shoe if one drove a car so curiously laden did not deter me. I decided to try it.

I got the sheet. To be accurate, it was a large tea-cloth, and it already had a number of small holes in it. Through these holes I passed the dahlias. I was so excited that it was not until I had put all the dahlias in that I suddenly realized that the tea-cloth was now the most beautiful thing I had ever seen. It was a flaming sheet of blossom. One could see hardly any cloth, and the stalks, of course, were invisible.

I hung the cloth in the car, pinning it to the roof with safety-pins, and departed to London. The experiment was completely successful. The dahlias were quite unharmed and lasted a week.

§ v i

However, that living sheet of blossom still glowed in my mind. It seemed to have endless possibilities. Why should one not take old velvets and faded

266

brocades, stretch them over bowls and boxes of water, and thread the stalks of flowers through them? Apart from the decorative value of the idea, it appealed to me because it was such a good way of using up flowers with short stalks. I have never been greatly attracted by flowers floating in a bowl of water. They always seem to look 'arty'. (Camellias in a black bowl are particularly revolting.) Besides, the petals get sodden and the water dusty, and the flowers never keep their position.

My first experiment was with a wide shallow tin box, about two feet square. I had it covered with an old piece of wine-coloured velvet. Then I picked a mass of deep red carnations. They were the old-fashioned carnations with quantities of buds, and stalks only about two inches long. I pushed the stalks through the velvet, and long before the job was done I had to rush out and get people to look at it, because it was so beautiful. I put the finished box on a very low miniature gate-leg table. It was so ravishingly lovely that my week-end party grew quite hysterical, and everybody began to make good resolutions, and swear eternal friendship, and that sort of thing.

This idea has now been considerably elaborated. And it has had one development of such charm that really I think somebody ought to put up a statue to me at the earliest possible opportunity. The idea is called:

THE LIVING FLOWER PICTURE

Imagine to yourself an old mantelpiece with a few bits of blue china and very worn pewter on it. Hanging above, in a plain gilt frame, is a picture of such brilliant colour that you instantly approach it to see by whom it is painted. And then you realize that it was painted by no human artist but by Nature. (You must take a deep breath after reading that last sentence, and try to look surprised.)

But in all seriousness, this is a charming conception. And it *works*. I have done it. I got a carpenter to knock some holes in my staircase wall. It was a very easy job, because they had to be only about six inches deep. The holes were made square and whitewashed. Then I had two plain gilt frames made to fit the holes, and stretched parchment-coloured velvet across the frames. Behind the frames I put a shallow glass bowl in each niche.

The first living flower picture I ever hung was made of my old friends, the dahlias. They are ideal flowers to use for this purpose because they have long stalks as well as short. The long stalks, naturally, you use for the top of the picture. They may be inclined to shoot out of the bowl, owing to the slight pressure on their necks, so that it is wise to put a wire net over the bowl. Nobody will see the bowl, so it does not matter.

You may think that all this is precious and tiresome. Please try not to think so, because if you try it I do swear that you will find many hours of happiness. Only I do not really advise arranging for the flower pictures to be on the staircase wall. They look so lovely, as you carry up your latest candle, that they may keep you out of bed for hours.

CHAPTER XVIII

A NOTE ON LONDON GARDENS

§ 1

POOLS and cupids and cats, and very crazy pavements, and seats that are scrubbed, on rare summer evenings, by sulky butlers. Tubs of startled scarlet geraniums, that have been popped into place a few hours before a cocktail party. A thin and wistful virginia creeper, whose autumn flush bears poignant witness to the metropolitan fever that devours it. Women in satin cloaks, drifting about on roof gardens, wondering if the clipped box standard affords sufficient conceal-ment to enable them to make pretty faces at some other woman's man. Starved wallflowers, trying vainly to shake the grime from their faces . . . gleam-ing a sickly gold after the city's rain, as though the breath of the fields had touched their faces. A con-sumptive rose hanging, frightened, outside a warm library. Plane trees singing overhead in Bloomsbury . . . carelessly rapturous . . . as though their grim background amused them . . . as though they welcomed the soot and the grime, in order that they might show, with the swifter arrogance, the pale and lovely flesh beneath the bark.

Men, coming and going, through the heated rooms into the dark chill outside, leaving a pleasant, healthy smell of sweat and earth behind them. In New York it is a question of 'Will the ivy be set by six? You see, we're spending a lot of money on these illuminations, and unless that ivy . . .' And the answer is always, 'Oh yeah . . . the ivy'll be O.K. by six . . . don't you worry . . . no *sir* . . . the ivy'll be O.K.' In London it is: 'I want some sort of display for the spring . . . I thought, perhaps . . . geraniums . . .?' And the answer is always 'Yes sir . . . nothing like geraniums . . . our Mr. Jones will call on you in due course.'

Which is a conventional picture of the average rich man's idea of a city garden. And since I have drawn it, there must needs be the equally conventional picture of the other sort of garden . . . the garden of the poor.

But here convention flies out of the window. For every poor man's garden, in a city, is a sweet but pitiful illustration of some faint striving after beauty, it shows his feeble groping for freedom — the freedom which he sees in even the faintest and weakest caprice of the vine that reaches so weakly, so painfully, towards his bedroom window. In these flowery prisons he finds release . . . sees visions in a window-box . . . escapes even, beneath the disheartened leaves that struggle up in a solitary flower-pot. I think that nothing is so sad nor yet so strangely inspiriting as the sight, in dark London alleys, of these green patches which are the nearest approach that some men will ever make to the fields so far away.

A NOTE ON LONDON GARDENS

This restless longing for a few green leaves, which lies always in the heart of very poor people, was once brought home to me, poignantly enough, by an old charwoman whom I once employed. We will call her Mrs. Heath. If you dislike sentimental stories you had better skip this section. I cannot tell it truly without seeming sentimental.

I was suffering from an acute attack of overdraft, economizing in a basement. (This was about the time when trees were being ordered for the wood at the rate of twenty a week.) However, though it was a basement, with hardly any sun, I rigged up some shelves outside the window and arranged a nice little display of green. There was, for example, a honey-suckle in a very small pot which flourished astonishingly. I was able to train its branches right up the grimy bars outside the window.

One day Mrs. Heath came to me, screwing the corner of her apron, and looking as though she had been detected in a crime.

'Oh sir!' she said. 'I've put a little pot on the shelf outside and I hope you won't mind.'

'A pot!'

'Yes sir. It's my own pot and I wanted it to get some air. It's got orange pips in it.'

'But do you think they'll grow there? There's hardly any sun.'

'There's a good deal more sun than where I lives, sir.'

'And what about the frosts?'

'We could put a piece of glass over them, sir.'

And so it was. As the year sped on I grew more and more interested in the orange pips. I would come home from the cottage, loaded with flowers, and filled with memories of a hundred excitements, and even before the flowers were put in water, a visit had to be paid to the back yard to see if the orange pips had started to grow.

Then one morning Mrs. Heath woke me up with a very smiling face.

'One's come through, sir,' she proclaimed proudly.

I had been dreaming of tigers trying to escape from a cage, and was startled. However, as soon as I realized what she meant, I put on a dressing-gown and hurried out. Yes, there it was — a tiny pale shoot, just showing.

'But they'll never flower, will they?'

'No, not in England, sir.'

'Well then. . . .'

'Not in England,' she repeated. Then she added, mysteriously, 'but in California they will.'

'But we're rather a long way from California.'

'Just now, we are, sir. 'Owever. . . .'

And then the secret came out. She had a daughter in California. Married to a young farmer. As soon as they were more settled she was going out to live with them. Her face lit up when she told me about her Ellen and the sunshine and the farm. She bustled into the kitchen and produced some postcards of the district in which Ellen lived. They were pretty postcards, showing enormous trees against skies of incredible blue.

This, it appeared, was the explanation of the orange pips.

'She's got a whole avenue of oranges, Ellen has,' said Mrs. Heath. 'But she 'asn't any *English* oranges! So I'm going to take these out to 'er as a surprise. Oh yes, they'll flower out there, in all that 'eat, and they'll fruit too . . . perhaps I'll be sending you a crate of 'em one of these days.'

She put away the postcards in her bag, smoothed her apron and became once again the respectful charwoman who 'knew her place,' and did not talk to the gentry. But as she went out of the room, loaded with the heavy tray, she added softly 'Somehow it makes me feel nearer to her, watching them pips grow. We're both looking forward to the sunshine. Me and the pips.'

But she never saw the sunshine. A few months later I moved into another house, and Mrs. Heath got another job. I saw her occasionally, when there was a little party and we wanted some extra help. But gradually I lost sight of her.

It must have been nearly two years afterwards that there was delivered at the cottage a very dilapidated parcel, tied up in sodden brown paper. There was some earth coming out of one of the corners, so I took it into the garden to open it. When I had unwrapped the paper there appeared a little heap of earth in which were twelve tiny orange plants. They had small shiny leaves and thin white roots. The pips from which they had sprung were still clearly visible.

Accompanying the parcel was a letter. It was from Mrs. Heath:

'Dear Sir,

'My Ellen died last week with her first baby. I got the telegram three days ago. Mrs. Thomas from next door has come in and put me to bed because I do not seem able to face things again just yet.

'I am sending you the little orange trees. I would not like to see them any more. Perhaps they may be flowering for you one day.

'I am, sir,
'Respectfully,
'Mrs. Heath.'

The orange trees have grown since then. They are fine sturdy plants with big glossy leaves.

But they have never flowered. Somehow, I hope they never will.

§ III

The first real London garden I ever had was in Chelsea. It was only about twenty feet by twelve, but it produced an astonishing variety of flowers.

During my first year I relied almost entirely upon penny packets, with the happiest results. Some of the packets did not even cost a penny, because of the charming custom which prevails with certain magazines of popular gardening, whose editors present their readers, week by week, with free packets of seeds throughout the spring. There was an extraordinary thrill in receiving these little presents. One read about them for weeks before. In thick black type one learnt that 'A Monster Packet of Crimson Flax will be Presented to every Purchaser of our Spring Number.' In the next issue, this information was reiterated, together with further particulars of the crimson flax . . . its elegance, its speed in growing, its amiability. In the penultimate issue, one's appetite was whetted almost cruelly, for here, splashed across the page in tints of blood, was the crimson flax's likeness . . . never, one felt, could any flower be lovelier, nor own so sweet a disposition.

Yet, there was still a whole week to wait! The fact that it would have been extremely simple to walk to the seedsman across the street, and buy enough crimson flax to sow a large part of Hyde Park, never occurred to one . . . or, if it did occur, was dismissed as an insulting idea. What was seed which was bought, compared to the packet which was about to be given? Nothing. Worse than nothing.

And then, it arrived at last! The little packet, that rattled when one shook it, glued to the outside cover of the magazine. It had to be peeled off very carefully, because the paper was thin, and it would be tragic if any of the seeds were spilt. How carefully those seeds were sown . . . with what infinite attention to the directions on the packet . . . in soil as sweet and sunny as offered itself.

Yes, they are clever men, the editors of those

magazines of popular gardening, for their gifts have a value out of all proportion to their market price. And often, as I have passed the bookstalls, where the newspapers and reviews and other periodicals are heaped high and glistening, I have paused, seen a pile of my favourite magazine, each with its packet of seeds glued to the cover, and have pondered on the miracle which lies there, the unborn beauty which is hidden among the rubbish-heap of trash — have longed for a magic wand that would cause those flowers to break into sudden blossom, and turn the news-stall into a flower-shop of crimson and green.

§ I V

Besides the annuals, I had several climbing roses, a lilac, and a beautiful syringa. It was an old syringa, and at first we thought it was dead, but it responded to care. However I had even more exciting things than that. For instance, foxgloves!

I have never seen foxgloves in any other London garden, and I cannot think why, because they do extremely well, particularly the white ones. They do not need much sun and they like a coarse soil. The one thing they hate is damp, especially when they are young. In order to avoid damp, I used, quite shame-lessly, to put umbrellas over my foxgloves on rainy afternoons and long wet nights. People thought it odd and affected, but I fail to see why it is affected to want to protect a lovely thing like a foxglove, especially when it is so very easy to do. I would always lend an umbrella to any woman who had left hers at home.

A NOTE ON LONDON GARDENS

I like foxgloves more than I like many women. Foxgloves cannot leave their umbrellas at home, because they haven't any umbrellas. Ergo. . . .

If you have a nice clump of foxgloves in your back garden you cannot ever be bored. There is the echo of all the sweet and liquid sounds of the country in their pale bells. In addition, I am told that their roots, if boiled and added to the soup, are guaranteed to make your most disagreeable enemy expire in considerable discomfort within twenty-four hours, but I have not tested this personally.

Pansies, of course, you must have. Only please do behave like a gentleman, or a lady, or whatever you are, with your pansies, i.e. *pick off every dead one.* It is monstrous — the way people neglect their pansies. To leave dead pansies on a plant is as cruel as leaving a cow without anybody to milk it. Also it is not only cruel, but foolish, because if you religiously pick off every flower the instant it is withered, you will be rewarded by flowers almost all the year round.

As soon as you plant a pansy in any town garden, about a thousand slugs will instantly appear from nowhere and begin to devour it. In destroying the slugs you will be able to pass a great many summer evenings very unpleasantly.

Other hardy herbaceous plants which can be recommended for town gardens, from my own experience, are:

Astrantia major
Campanula persicifolia
Funkia Sieboldiana

Lilium pardalinum
Pulmonaria angustifolia
Sedum spectabile

If you do not know what these are, and if you have been lulled into a trance by my easy-flowing style, you can do a little work yourself, for a change, and look them up in a dictionary.

(The somewhat acid tone of that last sentence was due to the fact that as I was making the list, a large and ravishing Persian cat was clearly visible in my back yard, patting my only geranium with a verve which would have been more fittingly reserved for a mouse.)

§v

Therefore we now come to cats. Or rather, cats come to us. These angelic creatures are bound to crop up, sooner or later, in any discussion of city gardens.

I adore cats. I do not mind them at all when they scrape their exquisite claws all down one's best arm-chair. I have not the heart to reprimand them when they push a cold, purring nose against an ornament and whisk it off my desk . . . because their expression of faint disdain as they regard the ornament, after it has been foolish enough to fall to the floor, is worth any ornament that was ever made. But in a small city garden, their charms, one is bound to admit, are not seen to the best advantage.

In my little Chelsea garden the walls were low and allowed a maximum of sunlight. However, the walls were also broad and supported a maximum of cats. It was soon evident that the boundary wall was the

recognized promenade for all the cats of Chelsea . . .
it was a sort of feline Piccadilly. Every day, towards
the hour of dusk, dark figures would emerge from
neighbouring scullery windows, stretch, yawn, and
take a sudden bound on to this wall. Having bounded,
they would proceed to saunter, with assumed nonchalance, in the direction of my little piece of wall.

As the shadows deepened, more and more of the
dark figures emerged. They hopped delicately from
the branches of trees. They appeared from sombre
doorways, their eyes catching the last glint of the
dying sun. Like tiny dots, they were seen in the
distance, as though they had fallen from the clouds.
And soon the whole wall was crowned with a stealthy
procession of arched backs and feathery tails, passing
to and fro, in a strange and ghostly saraband.

But it was not till they arrived at my particular
patch of wall that they deigned to break the silence,
to greet one another, to lift their voices in joy or in
pain. Why they always chose my little piece, I do not
know. Perhaps it was because there were trees in
each of the neighbouring gardens, which met and
formed a pleasant shelter. Perhaps it was because
my part of wall was, for some reason unknown, a little
wider than the rest. Whatever the reason, I found
that there was only one way to get rid of them. I
will tell you it in a moment.

First, however, I tried all the usual methods. I
tried opening the window and saying 'boo! damn!
shish!' followed by a scraping noise in the throat.
This appeared to please the cats greatly. A look of

dreamy ecstasy came into their eyes, and they gravely seated themselves, waiting for more. 'Hosh! Hell! Boo! Blast! Shish!' I yelled. Better and better, thought the cats. Their large green eyes widened, and though they occasionally examined their paws, to see that their nails were properly manicured, they soon resumed their rapt attention. 'Yah! Blast! Bang! Hish! Poo!' I shrieked. Then gradually the cats grew a little bored, decided that they had seen enough, yawned, got up and resumed their promenade, absently nibbling a little syringa as they went.

I also tried throwing things. However, since I should never have forgiven myself if I had hit a beautiful black cat (and should have felt even worse if I had hit an ugly one), and since, in addition, I could never have hit one even if I had tried, it cannot be said that this manœuvre was brilliantly successful.

Then I put wire netting over the seeds. It was instantly agreed, by all the cats in the district, that this was a most thoughtful act on my part. Wire netting, they averred, was the one amenity which hitherto they had lacked. They arrived in hordes to sit on it. Some of them bounced up and down on it as though it were a spring mattress. Others went fast asleep on it. When one went out into the back yard to remonstrate with them, they merely yawned, looked at one with shameless coquetry, and then turned over, with a gesture that said 'Leave, oh leave me to repose.'

Hell! Cats simply ought not to be allowed to go about, radiating such distracting charm.

But I solved the problem. The remedy sounds even sillier than the umbrellas over the foxgloves, but, heaven knows, it is too late in this book to trouble about being silly. For the remedy was *treacle*. Small pools of treacle, carefully poured on to the top of the wall, and renewed once a week. My original intention had been to scare the cats away altogether. They are the daintiest creatures, and I hoped that when they found themselves stepping into the sticky treacle they would shake their paws, sniff, and go back home. They would think me a common brute, but I could not help that.

However, they did not do what I expected them to do. (No cat ever does.) They approached my wall, stepped in the treacle, paused a moment in astonishment, and then hopped away to a little distance to lick their paws. For one reason or another, they no longer jumped down on to my flower beds.

I am sure that this all sounds very odd, and quite crazy. But it happens to be true.

§ VI

I wish that one could deal with garden 'ornaments' as easily as I dealt with the cats. But leaden cupids and little terra-cotta girls have a way of creeping in to the gardens of even the strongest-minded people. And once they have crept in, they seem to remain for ever.

The city garden shops are responsible for those monstrosities. There are one or two good garden shops in London and New York . . . shops where you can go in and tell them that you want a herbaceous border dug, and a plain brick path, and some trellis work for the wall at the end. And they will do what you ask, and no more.

But the average garden shop . . . give its proprietor half a chance, and before you know where you are your back yard will look like a Rhine-maiden's grotto, and it will be so full of ornaments that there will not be an inch left in which to grow any plants. You may weakly agree, at first, to buy one leaden cupid. The cupid will arrive, looking like a very horrible baby that has been petrified just as it was having an acute attack of wind. You think that perhaps if you get a quickly growing ivy you may be able to cover its revolting nakedness.

But you are mistaken. Your purchase of the cupid has caused your name to be entered in the books of the gardening firm as a 'sucker'. The proprietor will sit in his shop, rubbing his hands and licking his lips, and he will remember all the other horrors they have on hand, in their cellars and attics. That terra-cotta stork, for example, that was made in Czecho-slovakia, and should have been allowed to stay there. It has green eyes, and it stands on a cement log, tinted, oh so cunningly, to resemble the real wood! And the bird-bath, which is made of imitation marble, and has four wrought-iron sparrows perched on the brim (evidently about to be sick into the basin, if you will join me in a little coarseness). And the very, very, *very* whimsical German manikins, that look more and more frightful, however much you move them about. And the imitation Italian plaques, that look so like 'the real thing' (whatever that may be), especially after they have been subjected to a few months' London grime.

And — of course — the rustic seat, with the little poem carved on the back. They are quite determined that you must have *that*. After all, it serves so many purposes, does it not? It is 'artistic' — of that there can be no doubt, for it is listed in the wholesale catalogues under 'Art, Accessories, etc.' It is also useful, for as soon as you sit down on it, the neighbours can have a really good glare at you through their windows, instead of having to bob their heads up and down to see what you are doing to the nasturtiums. And it is extremely inspiring. For naturally we all like to be reminded that a garden is a lovesome thing God 'wot' . . . or is it 'which'?

§ V I I

But no . . . I should not make fun of that poem. It may have been beautiful before the anthologists seized upon it. And I have not the heart to sneer at any man who offers his thanks to God for a garden, even if the garden is a backyard. No — most of all *because* it is a backyard.

For city gardens have a strange magic which is quite their own. You stand in your little plot. All around you are houses, chimney pots, windows, smoke. For mile upon mile, you know, there are bald, blank streets, in which no blade of grass will grow. They are so far away, the green fields, that you feel you may never see them again . . . you are trapped, like a prisoner, in a cell . . . a cell whose horror is accentuated by the fact that its door is unlocked . . . so that you may escape . . . but escape into what? Into another cell, and yet another, until you begin to run madly, down streets that never end, until you fall exhausted at the foot of a lamp-post, on a hard pavement.

Yet here, before you, is a growing rose. Green and proud and sweet. It is as though its leaves were luminous, such infinite comfort do they exhale as they climb up the sombre brick. All around the rose, in the dark earth, are tiny sprouts and delicate leaves, that proclaim a gracious independence of civilization. Why, when the wind comes, there is even a rustle in the leaves, so that if you close your eyes you can fancy yourself in the country. But you do not wish to close your eyes. You want to see what the rose is doing . . . guess its plans . . . to learn its pattern by heart. And then, suddenly, you realize what the rose *is* doing.

It is becoming covered with blight.

Now the proper thing to do, for those people who think that a 'laugh' is of paramount importance, at all moments of life, is, most emphatically, to giggle at the sentence which I have put in italics. If a writer ends any prettily woven passage with a clumsy knot of words . . . or, to put it otherwise, if he steps out of his shadow of fantasy into the crude gas-light of common sense . . . what can a self-respecting reader do but laugh? Or, if he doesn't think it funny, to yawn and nibble the olive which reposed at the bottom of his bronx.

Yet, I didn't want you to laugh at the line about the blight. Is it a terrible confession of failure to say that? I suppose it is. I imagine — a little doubtfully — that a great artist in words should be able to interpose, with unerring effect, his slabs of comedy and 'pathos' — as elegantly as the chefs in New York who surround a brittle ice-cream with a molten *soufflé*, and keep the two apart.

Yet perhaps you felt as I did about the blight . . . that it was rather wonderful, and that it had a certain beauty, in its context. I am not suggesting that we must not, quite ruthlessly, destroy it . . . that we must not take a deep breath, extend the thumb and fore-finger, and squash the horrible little green insects who have arrived from limbo, to play havoc with the rose. What I *am* suggesting — with quite tedious prolixity — is that there is a real miracle in the appearance of the blight at all. From what far caverns of pestilence did it come? What power invested these pallid, sickly insects, that they should fly over miles of arid slate (if that is how it is done) through the acrid fumes of a million hostile chimneys, over the dangerous turbulence of countless crowded streets, in search of your one rose-tree?

That is the miracle. Perhaps some one will explain it for me. And yet, however it is explained, I shall never quite lose my sense of awe, as each spring I stand in my tiny garden, with the roof towering above me, and see the blight on my rose tree. For the blight knows that my rose really *is* a rose, as good as any rose that ever flowered in the coloured counties. And so do I.

EPILOGUE

This is a book to which there can be no ending. No sooner is a line drawn, and Finis written, than a spray of blossom flings its shadow across the page, a faint perfume drifts through the open window, and the mind is off again, down flowery lanes of memory.

I have written Finis, and since I am sitting at a desk in London, on a foggy December evening, with all the windows tightly shut, it would seem that no scent could assail, no shadow lure me from the goal. Yet — and this is a phenomenon which I believe all garden lovers will have observed — the garden is *here* . . . in this room . . . with all its flowers and leaves about me, and all its paths glimmering in the dusk.

A gardener is never shut out from his garden, wherever he may be. Its comfort never fails. Though the city may close about him, and the grime and soot descend upon him, he can still wander in his garden, does he but close his eyes. A clumsy paraphrase, you will tell me, of the lines: 'stone walls do not a prison make, nor iron bars a cage.'

Yet the paraphrase is worth making, because it *is* so very singular — this power which we have of transporting ourselves, at will, to our gardens. I have sometimes mentioned, to other gardeners, a little diffidently, my own capacities in this direction, and they see nothing strange in it, for they have the same talents themselves. Were it not for their assurance I might feel that I was going mad.

For, on sleepless nights, I can close my eyes and lie, very quietly in my London bedroom, and enjoy my garden almost as keenly as though I were in it. Indeed, the fantasy is in some ways more charming than the reality, for now the seasons are at my beck and call. Which shall it be — spring or autumn? Shall I have a daffodil morning, with the wind blowing keen through the yellow drifts, or shall I stand quite still on a misty October evening, with a haze of Michaelmas daisies around me, and no sound save the fall of a chestnut in a distant grove? The clock of Time, in these quiet night hours, is here to be switched as you will, and however you may choose to move it, the hands will point the way to loveliness. Shut your eyes a little tighter and it is iris time — their brilliant blues dazzle you — in their azure depths the dewdrops gleam like sapphires; why, you can almost count the hairs on each delicate tongue, so keen is your vision.

I turn in my bed . . . sleep is somewhere round the corner . . . but whether one wakes or dreams . . . what does it matter? For here, in an unearthly breeze, the snowdrops are swaying . . . never were they whiter . . . never did their poignant innocence so sweetly proclaim itself. And the very walls of the room seem to twinkle with the yellow stars of the jasmine . . . and somewhere . . . ah! the clock has shifted again . . . somewhere, far, far away, there is the scent of lilac. . . .

EPILOGUE

And then sleep comes.

And thus, without doubt, it will come to my little group of patient readers, do I not make an end . . . .

The end must therefore be made . . . and it is an agonizing business, to say good-bye to a garden. Often, when the car has been panting outside in the lane, I have run back for one last look . . . there was a lily I had forgotten . . . or a bluebell that was almost blue . . . or a rose that was in hiding, among the quiet shadows on the wall. Desperately I run out, while the car chug-chugs in the distance. The peace of the garden descends upon me. The green leaves enfold me. Time, and the car, they are both forgotten. Was it a lily I was seeking? The sweet earth trembles with lilies unborn. A bluebell that was still faintly tinged with the green of Nature's adolescence? Why . . . the sky is a field of bluebells above me . . . this is the time to lie back and wander lazily among them.

A rose, in the shadows? Yes . . . indeed . . . for all the shadows teem with roses . . . there are ghostly crimsons and phantom purples, yellows unborn and whites of an innocence unknown; there are reds so radiant that the brain is bewildered, and over them all drifts a fragrance that is sweeter than love itself. . . .

Thus does one dream . . . and stray . . . and dream . . . and stray. But always there is the waiting car. We must not keep the car waiting. I must lay aside my pen. You must send this book back to the library. And I hope you get a good Edgar Wallace in exchange, a book in which something really *happens*.

But I warn you, I am going to write at least six more gardening books. They will be thrust upon you, by cunning maidens, under titles which will make you think that they have nothing to do with gardening at all. But they will have everything to do with gardening.

For, as I observed, in the foreword to this little book, 'a garden is the only mistress who never fades, who never fails.'

INDEX

This index of plant names was prepared by Roy C. Dicks. Scientific names have been corrected and updated where necessary.

Abies concolor (Colorado fir), 163
Acacia baileyana (golden mimosa, wattle), 58–61, 218–219, 225
Acer (maple), 175, 177
   A. dasycarpum [now *A. saccharinum*] (silver maple), 163
Aconite, winter. See *Eranthis*
Aesculus hippocastanum (horse chestnut), 163, 177, 178
Alcea (hollyhock), 35, 55, 132
Almond. See *Prunus dulcis*
Alyssum, 116
Anagallis (pimpernel), 91–93
   A. arvensis (scarlet pimpernel), 222
Anemone, 152, 216, 217
   A. hupehensis var. *japonica* (Japanese anemone), 83, 189, 254
Araucaria araucana (monkey puzzle tree), 122

Ash tree. See *Fraxinus*
Aster, 198
   A. novi-belgii (Michaelmas daisy), 56, 83, 254, 288
Astrantia major, 277
Aubrieta (aubretia), 124, 128–129

Barberry, Japanese. See *Berberis japonica*
Beech. See *Fagus*
Berberis japonica (Japanese barberry), 77
Betula pendula (silver or cutleaf birch), 162, 163
Birch, silver or cutleaf. See *Betula pendula*
Blackberry. See *Rubus*
Blackthorn. See *Prunus spinosa*
Bluebell. See *Hyacinthoides*
Borago officinalis (burrage), 216
Boxwood. See *Buxus*

Broom. See *Cytisus*

Burrage. See *Borago officinalis*

Buxus (boxwood), 269

Calandrinia umbellata (rock purslane), 130

Campanula persicifolia, 277

Carnation. See *Dianthus caryophyllus*

Castanea (chestnut), 23, 146, 176

Cedrus (cedar), 165

Celastrus (spindle), 152

Cheiranthus cheiri (wallflower), 40, 94–95, 102, 260, 261, 262, 269

Cherry. See *Prunus*

Chestnut. See *Castanea*

Chimonathus fragrans (wintersweet), 64, 68

Chionodoxa (glory of the snow), 124–128

Christmas rose. See *Helleborus niger*

Chrysanthemum, 54, 56, 241, 254, 261

Cineraria, 215–216, 218

Cistus (rock rose), 116, 216

Citrus aurantiifolia (lime), 162, 176

C. sinensis (orange), 271–274

Clematis, 250, 251–252

Colorado Douglas fir. See *Pseudotsuga menziesii* subsp. *glauca*

Consolida (larkspur), 189, 260, 262

Coreopsis, 189

Corylopsis spicata (spike witch hazel), 76

Corylus avellana (hazelnut), 140

C. maxima 'Halle'sche Riesennuss' ('Merveille de Bollwyller'; filbert), 163

Cosmos, 188, 241, 250

Cowslip. See *Primula veris*

Crab apple. See *Malus sylvestris*

Crataegus (hawthorn; may; thorn), 20, 163

C. pyracantha [now *Pyracantha coccinea*] (firethorn), 161–162

Creeping Jenny. See *Lysimachia nummularia*

Crocus, 20, 145

C. imperati, 71–73

C. sieberi, 73

Cupressus (cypress), 174

Cyclamen, 95, 213–215, 216, 218

C. coum, 77, 213

Cypress. See *Cupressus*

Cytisus (broom), 176, 178

Daffodil. See *Narcissus*

Dahlia, 84, 95, 189, 195, 265–266, 268

Daisy (indeterminate genus), 216, 261, 262

Daisy, Michaelmas. See *Aster novi-belgii*

Damson. See *Prunus domestica*

Dandelion. See *Taraxacum*

Daphne mezereum, 73–74

Delphinium, 38, 95, 250

Deutzia, 249

Dianthus caryophyllus (carnation), 267

Digitalis (foxglove), 276–267

Dock. See *Rumex*

Elderberry. See *Sambucus*
Elm tree. See *Ulmus*
Eranthis (winter aconite), 62–64, 68
Erica carnea (winter heather), 68–69
Exochorda grandiflora [now *E. racemosa*] (pearlbush), 176

Fagus (beech), 23
Filbert. See *Corylus maxima* 'Halle'sche Riesennuss' ('Merveille de Bollwyller')
Fir, Colorado. See *Abies concolor*
Firethorn. See *Crataegus pyracantha* [now *Pyracantha coccinea*]
Flax. See *Linum*
Forget-me-not. See *Myosotis*
Forsythia ×*intermedia*, 77
Foxglove. See *Digitalis*
Fraxinus (ash), 165–166
Freesia, 74
Fuchsia, 131, 199

Galanthus (snowdrop), 25, 40, 42, 55, 251, 260, 264–265, 288
G. *elwesii*, 78–79
Geranium, 131, 199, 258, 269, 270
Glory of the snow. See *Chionodoxa*
Gourd, 47
Grape vine. See *Vitis vinifera*
Groundsel. See *Senecio vulgaris*
Guelder rose. See *Viburnum opulus*

Hamamelis mollis (witch-hazel), 40, 65–67, 68
Hawthorn (may). See *Crataegus*
Hazelnut. See *Corylus avellana*
Hazelnut 'Merveille de Bollwyller'. See *Corylus maxima* 'Halle'sche Riesennuss'
Heather, winter. See *Erica carnea*
Hedera (ivy), 26, 134, 136, 137, 178, 270, 282
Heliotropium, 220
Helleborus niger (Christmas rose), 51, 52, 54, 55, 56, 77–78
Holly. See *Ilex*
Hollyhock. See *Alcea*
Honeysuckle. See *Lonicera*
Horse chestnut. See *Aesculus hippocastanum*
Hosta sieboldiana [formerly *Funkia sieboldiana*], 277
Hyacinthoides (bluebell, hyacinth), 51, 95, 289

Ilex (holly), 184
Ionopsidium acaule (violet cress), 62
Iris, 254, 288
   I. stylosa [now *I. unguicularis*] (winter iris), 70–71, 84
Ivy. See *Hedera*

Jasminum (jasmine), 134, 136, 145, 194–195, 250, 288
   J. nudiflorum (winter jasmine), 52, 54, 55, 56, 65, 94

Juglans regia (walnut), 163

Kniphofia (redhot poker), 252–256

Laburnum, 162, 219
Larkspur. See *Consolida*
Lathyrus odoratus (sweetpea), 212, 223
Laurel. See *Prunus laurocerasus*
Laurustinus. See *Viburnum tinus*
Lavandula (lavender), 42, 96, 226
Lilac. See *Syringa*
Lilium (lily), 95, 133, 258, 289
  L. candidum (madonna lily), 16, 250
  L. pardalinum (leopard lily), 277
Lime. See *Citrus aurantiifolia*
Linum (flax), 216, 275
Liriodendron tulipifera (tulip tree), 185
Lonicera (honeysuckle), 99, 134, 250, 271
  L. fragrantissima (winter honeysuckle), 74–75
Lungwort. See *Pulmonaria angustifolia*
Lupinus (lupin), 48–50, 75, 99
Lychnis flos-cuculi (ragged robin), 222
Lysimachia nummularia (creeping Jenny), 237

Malus sylvestris (crab apple), 176
Maple. See *Acer*

Maple, silver. See *Acer dasycarpum*
Marigold. See *Tagetes*
Matthiola (stock), 95, 260
May (hawthorn). See *Crataegus*
Meconopsis (poppy), 38
Mimosa, golden. See *Acacia baileyana*
Mimulus (monkey flower), 199
Mistletoe. See *Viscum album*
Mock orange. See *Philadelphus*
Monkey flower. See *Mimulus*
Monkey puzzle tree. See *Araucaria araucana*
Mountain ash. See *Sorbus aucuparia*
Mushrooms, 43–46
Myosotis (forget-me-not), 212

Narcissus (daffodil), 25, 228–229, 248, 288
  N. papyraceus (paper-white narcissus), 264
Nasturtium. See *Tropaeolum*
Nemesia, 212

Oak. See *Quercus*
Ophelia [now *Swertia*], 249
Orange. See *Citrus sinensis*
Orchis (orchid), 65, 220–221, 232

Pansy. See *Viola*
Parthenocissus quinquefolia (Virginia creeper), 269
Pearlbush. See *Exochorda grandiflora*

Pelargonium graveolens (rose geranium), 145–150
Periwinkle. See *Vinca*
Petasites fragrans (winter heliotrope), 69–70
Philadelphus (mock orange), 178, 187
Pimpernel. See *Anagallis*
Pinus (pine), 124
  P. nigra (Austrian pine), 163
  P. sylvestris (Scotch [Scots] pine), 113
Platanus (plane, sycamore), 163, 174, 175, 269
Poplar. See *Populus*
Poppy. See *Meconopsis*
Populus (poplar), 41, 175
Primula (primrose), 25, 56, 65
  P. veris (cowslip), 76, 77
Prunus (cherry), 176, 177, 178
  P. domestica (damson), 17
  P. dulcis (almond), 140, 176
  P. laurocerasus (laurel), 122, 135, 138, 228
  P. spinosa (blackthorn), 40
Pseudotsuga menziesii subsp. *glauca* (Colorado Douglas fir), 163
Pulmonaria angustifolia (lungwort), 277

Quercus (Oak), 40, 175

Ragged robin. See *Lychnis floscuculi*
Redhot poker. See *Kniphofia*

Rhododendron, 42
Rock rose. See *Cistus*
Rock purslane. See *Calandrinia umbellata*
Rosa (rose), 16, 25–26, 35, 36, 41, 83, 85, 88, 95, 226, 233, 242, 260, 262, 269, 276, 284–286, 289
  R. rubiginosa (sweet briar), 41, 56, 90, 100, 105, 110, 134, 205–207
  R. moyseii, 163, 192
Rose geranium. See *Pelargonium graveolens*
Rubus (blackberry), 261
Rumex (dock), 124–125, 193, 234

Salix (Willow), 23, 161, 166–169, 174, 178
Sambucus (elderberry), 91
Saxifraga, 105, 116, 123, 231
  S. ciliata [now *Bergenia ciliata*], 77
  S. grisebachii [now *S. federiciaugusti* subsp. *grisebachii*], 129–130
Schizanthus, 212, 223
Sedum spectabile, 277
Senecio vulgaris (groundsel), 36, 85, 234
Snowball tree. See *Viburnum plicatum*
Snowdrop. See *Galanthus*
Sorbus aucuparia (mountain ash), 162, 177, 178, 183

Speedwell. See *Veronica*

Spike witch-hazel. See *Corylopsis spicata*

Spindle. See *Celastrus*

Spiraea, 183

Sternbergia lutea (winter daffodil), 76

Stock. See *Matthiola*

Sweet briar. See *Rosa rubiginosa*

Sweetpea. See *Lathyrus odoratus*

Sycamore (plane). See *Platanus*

Syringa (lilac), 17, 20, 38, 261, 276, 288

Tagetes (marigold), 261

T. tenuifolia (dwarf marigold), 230

Taraxacum (dandelion), 232, 260

Taxus (yew), 174, 255

Thorn (hawthorn). See *Crataegus*

Tropaeolum (nasturtium), 283

Tulip tree. See *Liriodendron tulipifera*

Ulmus (elm), 40, 135, 136, 162, 170, 175, 176, 178, 210

Veronica (speedwell), 222

Vetch, purple. See *Vicia Americana*

Viburnum opulus (guelder rose), 178

V. plicatum (snow ball tree), 186–187

V. tinus (laurustinus), 56

Vicia americana (purple vetch), 222

Vinca (periwinkle), 51

Viola (pansy, violet), 36, 56, 105, 116, 123, 133, 152, 238, 261, 277

Violet cress. See *Ionopsidium acaule*

Virginia creeper. See *Parthenocissus quinquefolia*

Viscum album (mistletoe), 145

Vitis vinifera (grape vine), 133–139, 192

Wallflower. See *Cheiranthus cheiri*

Walnut. See *Juglans regia*

Wattle (golden mimosa). See *Acacia baileyana*

Weeds, 85

Willow. See *Salix*

Winter daffodil. See *Sternbergia lutea*

Winter heliotrope. See *Petasites fragrans*

Wintersweet. See *Chimonathus fragrans*

Wisteria, 36, 99–100, 242, 250

Witch-hazel. See *Hamamelis mollis*

Yew. See *Taxus*

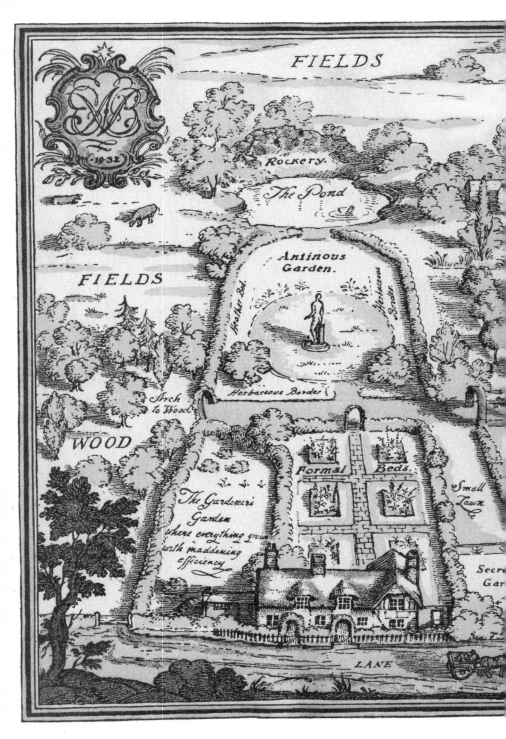

FIELDS

ROCKERY.

The Pond

Antinous
Garden.

Wall Bed

Herbaceous Border

FIELDS

Herbaceous Border

Arch
to Wood

WOOD

The Gardener's
Garden
where everything grows
with maddening
efficiency

Formal Beds.

Small
Lawn

Secret
Gar

LANE

1932